To a wonderful woman:

Colleen V.

From:

Donna B.

Date:

September 1, 2014

D1368085

Words of Jesus for
Women

Carolyn Larsen

CHRISTIAN ART
PUBLISHERS

Words of Jesus for Women

Published by Christian Art Publishers
· PO Box 1599, Vereeniging, 1930, RSA

© 2014
First edition 2014

Cover designed by Christian Art Publishers

Images used under license from Shutterstock.com

Unless otherwise indicated, all Scripture quotations
are taken from the *Holy Bible*, New International Version® NIV®.
Copyright © 1973, 1978, 1984, 2011 by International Bible Society.
Used by permission of Zondervan Publishing House.
All rights reserved.

Scripture quotations marked NLT are taken from the
Holy Bible, New Living Translation®, second edition.
Copyright © 1996, 2004 by Tyndale House Publishers,
Inc., Carol Stream, Illinois 60188.
All rights reserved.

Set in 11 on 14 pt Palatino LT Std
by Christian Art Publishers

Printed in China

ISBN 978-1-4321-0718-5

14   15   16   17   18   19   20   21   22   23   –   10   9   8   7   6   5   4   3   2   1

"As the Father
has loved Me,
so have I loved you.
Now remain in
My love."

~ John 15:9 ~

January

Difficult People

"Do to others as you would have them do to you."
~ LUKE 6:31

A simple command, right? It's so basic – treat other people the way you want them to treat you … with kindness, respect and honesty.

The interesting thing about Jesus' words here is that they come in the middle of instructions on how to treat people you may not really like – people who rub you the wrong way, people who perhaps just aren't nice, people with whom niceness is difficult.

Let's face it, treating your friends with kindness is not tough; treating the others with kindness … well, that's the Jesus way to live.

Living it

No act of kindness, no matter how small, is ever wasted.
– Aesop

Priorities

"What good is it for someone to gain the whole world, and yet lose or forfeit their very self?"

~ LUKE 9:25

This verse issues a challenge to honestly examine your life. You may confidently say, "God is most important in my life, of course." But is it really true?

Think about how you spend your time and energy every day. Is time with God the first thing pushed aside when life is busy? Does the focus to earn more money or accumulate more stuff or gain a higher position take precedence?

If knowing, loving and serving God is really most important, then spending time with Him, getting to know Him better and studying His Word should be your priority. If it isn't, confess it now and ask God's forgiveness. Make Him your number one priority.

Living it

Dear Father,
I have often spoken the words that You are the most important thing in my life, but I confess that there are times when my behavior does not bear out the conviction of those words. Forgive me, Father. Help me to get my priorities in line and give You the place of honor in my heart.

In Jesus' name, Amen.

A Critical Spirit

"Why do you look at the speck of sawdust in your brother's eye and pay no attention to the plank in your own eye?"
~ MATTHEW 7:3

*T*he sad thing is that a person who has a critical spirit can't seem to see her own issues – only the faults of others. She'll find something to criticize about pretty much everyone and she is not a very fun person to be around.

Jesus' words are a challenge to get real and not let yourself be one of those critical women. Be honest with yourself and deal with your own issues instead of criticizing others.

Every woman is responsible for her own choices. So, don't criticize someone else's behavior but ignore or justify your own.

Living it

Search me, God, and know my heart; test me and know my anxious thoughts. See if there is any offensive way in me, and lead me in the way everlasting.
– Psalm 139:23-24

All You Need

"When you give to the needy, do not let your left hand know what your right hand is doing, so that your giving may be in secret."

~ Matthew 6:3-4

It feels good to help someone in need. Maybe it feels so good that you want to talk about it. But, when you talk about it then attention is drawn to you and it becomes a sort of "pat yourself on the back" scenario ... even if you didn't intend it that way.

Jesus takes the pride out of helping others by encouraging you to do good deeds, but to keep quiet about what you've done.

Take joy in the fact that *you* know what you did ... and so does Jesus. That's all that's important.

Living it

A man wrapped up in himself makes a very small bundle.

– Benjamin Franklin

God's Love for You

"For God so loved the world that He gave His one and only Son, that whoever believes in Him shall not perish but have eternal life."

~ JOHN 3:16

This is probably the most well known verse in the Bible. In fact, you may know it so well that you just breeze through it without really thinking about the power in these words.

Jesus spoke these words to Nicodemus, a religious leader who no doubt knew the Scriptures but didn't understand what Jesus came to do. Take time to read this verse and think about every phrase. These words are filled with God's love for you.

Living it

Have you asked Jesus to be your Savior? Do you remember the day and the situation? Did someone pray with you or were you alone with the Lord? If you haven't invited Jesus into your heart, would you consider doing so now? John 3:16 tells what He has done for you.

Number One

"Anyone who wants to be first must be the very last, and the servant of all."

~ MARK 9:35

Jesus' words here are counter to pretty much every-thing the world counts as success. By Jesus' measure-ment of success there is no room for pride. He says to think of what's best for others before thinking of yourself. He says to serve others, not walk all over them.

This servant mentality may not make you a success in some people's eyes but it sure does in Jesus' eyes. That's most important anyway, right?

Living it

Be silent as to services you have rendered, but speak of favors you have received.

– Seneca

One on One

"If your brother or sister sins, go and point out their fault, just between the two of you. If they listen to you, you have won them over."

~ Matthew 18:15

$\mathcal{A}$ friend hurts you. If your first response is to tell someone else about it and garner support … well, you're not taking the Jesus route.

Jesus says that the first thing you should do is go to the person who has hurt you and see if you can work things out together. If you talk about the situation with others, then your friends choose sides and more problems are created. Keep it personal.

Living it

Brothers and sisters, if someone is caught in a sin, you who live by the Spirit should restore that person gently. But watch yourselves, or you also may be tempted. Carry each other's burdens, and in this way you will fulfill the law of Christ.

– Galatians 6:1-2

A Clean, Pure Heart

"Blessed are the pure in heart, for they will see God."

~ MATTHEW 5:8

*W*hat does it mean to be pure in heart? Purity suggests cleanliness; something that has not been even slightly dirtied.

The problem is that you were born with a sinful heart, so how can it be made pure? The only way to clean a sinful heart is by confessing your sin to Jesus and asking forgiveness. His sacrifice paid the price for your sin, and He will wash your heart clean. Keep your heart focused on God.

Living it

Dear Father,

Confession doesn't come easily to me because I get lost in all I need to confess. Father, make my sins visible to me so that I may bring them to You for confession. Help me to truly repent and turn away. Lord, help me to keep my heart focused on You.

In Jesus' name, Amen.

Jesus Came for All

"It is not the healthy who need a doctor, but the sick. I have not come to call the righteous, but sinners."
~ MARK 2:17

D o you hang around with people who are like you? People who believe like you do and have the same standards and lifestyle? OK, be honest – do people who are different kind of scare you? Do they make you uncomfortable? Of course you believe that all people need to hear about Jesus, but do you secretly hope that someone else will tell them?

What would it take for you to get out of your comfort zone a little so that you can be a living example of Jesus' love and care to those who need it?

Living it

The Great Commission is not an option to be considered; it is a command to be obeyed.
– Hudson Taylor

God Alone

Jesus answered, "It is written: 'Worship the Lord your God and serve Him only.'"

~ LUKE 4:8

You would never intentionally worship someone or something other than God, right? It happens so slowly that some thing or activity or person begins to take your time, attention and money, and suddenly your priorities are upside down. It's a slow slide down a slippery path that pulls you away from God.

This verse is Jesus' response when Satan tempted Jesus to worship him instead of God. Be alert to where your time and energy are going. Stay focused on knowing and worshiping God.

Living it

Sing to the LORD a new song; sing to the LORD, all the earth. Sing to the LORD, praise His name; proclaim His salvation day after day. Declare His glory among the nations, His marvelous deeds among all peoples. For great is the LORD and most worthy of praise; He is to be feared above all gods.

– Psalm 96:1-4

Stop Worrying

"Do not let your hearts be troubled. You believe in God; believe also in Me."

~ JOHN 14:1

Worry. Not worrying can be a challenge. You worry because you care so much. You worry because situations come where you aren't in control. You worry because you don't know the ending that's coming. You worry because you can't "fix" things for yourself or those you love.

The problem with worry is that you can't trust God and worry at the same time. Worry pushes aside trust. So, if you know Jesus loves you; if you believe what His word teaches, then ask Him to help you trust instead of worrying.

Living it

Every evening I turn my worries over to God. He's going to be up all night anyway.
– Mary C. Crowley

Worrying is like a rocking chair. It gives you something to do, but it gets you nowhere.
– Glen Turner

The Importance of Forgiveness

"When you stand praying, if you hold anything against any-one, forgive them, so that your Father in heaven may forgive you your sins."

~ MARK 11:25

Jesus puts a great deal of importance on relationships. He often encourages His followers to love others, think about others' feelings, and care for others. So the possibility of coming to Jesus in prayer, with your worship, praise and requests, when you are angry with another person, does not sit well with Him. Forgive others before you ask to be forgiven yourself.

Living it

Dear Father,

Why is forgiveness sometimes so hard for me? Someone has hurt me and I simply can't let it go. Yet I know that I must, because I ask Your forgiveness for my shortcomings. Help me, Father, to let go of my hurt. Father, fill my heart with compassion and love and forgiveness.

In Jesus' name, Amen.

Waiting for Light

"I am the light of the world. Whoever follows Me will never walk in darkness, but will have the light of life."
~ JOHN 8:12

*W*ouldn't it be cool to have a lighted path in front of you that showed you where to go and what to do? You do, you know!

Jesus is the light of the world. Staying close to Him, reading His Word and praying means that your path will be lit.

Does that mean you always know exactly what to do at any given moment? No. It does mean that if you wait, He will guide you. If you rush ahead – making decisions and choices on your own – you'll end up in darkness.

Living it

You, LORD, keep my lamp burning; my God turns my darkness into light.
– Psalm 18:28

Be Still and Listen

"When he has brought out all his own, he goes on ahead of them, and his sheep follow him because they know his voice."

~ John 10:4

Perhaps you've had the experience of being in a crowd of people and hearing a loved one call your name. How did you pick out that one voice from the cacophony of noise? It's a voice you love.

Do you recognize Jesus' voice in the noise of life? How do you know which voice in your mind is that of the Good Shepherd? You learn to know His voice by hearing it. You hear it by listening. You can only listen when you are quiet. Be still and listen for the Shepherd's voice. The more you hear it, the easier it will be to recognize it.

Living it

"Be still, and know that I am God; I will be exalted among the nations, I will be exalted in the earth."

– Psalm 46:10

Be still before the LORD, all mankind, because He has roused Himself from His holy dwelling.

– Zechariah 2:13

Knee-Jerk Reactions

"If someone slaps you on one cheek, turn to them the other also. If someone takes your coat, do not withhold your shirt from them."

~ LUKE 6:29

Reactions. Revenge. Anger. These emotions may just show the condition of your heart. When someone hurts you, what's your response? The knee-jerk reaction may be to strike back, but if you can pull that in and respond with patience and love, you will be responding as Jesus instructed.

Give others a chance to improve their own behavior and you will preserve relationships from being damaged. Remember that Jesus also said to love your neighbor as you love yourself, so reign in your reaction and try to see why someone behaves as they do. Let them see Jesus' love in your response.

Living it

Speak when you are angry – and you'll make the best speech you'll ever regret.

– Laurence J. Peter

Blending In

"You are the salt of the earth. But if the salt loses its saltiness, how can it be made salty again? It is no longer good for anything, except to be thrown out and trampled underfoot."

~ MATTHEW 5:13

It's tempting sometimes to blend in. It's just easier to not rock the boat, to not stand out in the crowd, to not draw attention to yourself.

Sometimes it's OK to blend in … but sometimes it isn't. The very fact that you are a Christ-follower means that there will be times when you must stand out, because "you are the salt of the earth." Your presence – which represents Christ's presence – will mean that you are the voice of love, peace and reason sometimes. Don't lose your saltiness.

Living it

Think of an occasion when you were salt to the world around you. If that hasn't happened yet, was there a time when you observed someone else being salt? How were either of these "salt experiences" received?

Future Foundation

"I am the resurrection and the life. The one who believes in Me will live, even though they die; and whoever lives by believing in Me will never die."
~ JOHN 11:25-26

A foundational promise for our Christian faith is the promise that Christ-followers will live forever with Him in eternity. God has power over death, which He proved when He raised Jesus back to life.

This doesn't mean that it isn't hard to lose a loved one. Grief may fill your heart, but your hope is in this promise from Jesus that our last breath on this earth is not the end. Believing in Jesus means eternity with Him and a glorious reunion with our loved ones who also belong to Him!

Living it

Dear Father,
I've lost loved ones to death, and I miss them. It was hard to say goodbye. Help me remember that there will one day be a joyful reunion in heaven. Thank You, Father, that You have victory over death! I can't wait for heaven!
In Jesus' name, Amen.

This Is What Matters

"Love the Lord your God with all your heart and with all your soul and with all your mind and with all your strength."

~ MARK 12:30

Don't blow by this verse, even though that might be easy to do because it's so familiar. You read it and think, "Well, of course I totally love God." Remember that Exodus 20:5 states that God is a jealous God. He wants your total devotion. Jesus restates that here.

It won't work to try and divide your devotion, worship or attention. God will not share your heart with any thing or any one. You're either all in or all out. You can try to worship and obey halfway, but you won't be fooling God. You won't be pleasing Him either.

Make an honest evaluation of what's important to you. Is there anything in your life that ranks above God?

Living it

"You shall not make for yourself an image in the form of anything in heaven above or on the earth beneath or in the waters below. You shall not bow down to them or worship them; for I, the LORD your God, am a jealous God."

– Exodus 20:4-5

The Second Most Important Command

"The second is this: 'Love your neighbor as yourself.' There is no commandment greater than these."
~ MARK 12:31

*D*on't rush by this verse either. Look at the disclaimer Jesus gave – there is no greater commandment than this one and the one just before it when He said that the *most* important commandment is to love God with all your heart. You can almost hear that Jesus spoke them in one breath. Love others. It's important.

The foundation of much of Jesus' teaching is loving others; respecting others; honoring others over yourself. It's imperative.

Are there things – behaviors or attitudes – in your life that you need to change in order to be obedient to this command? Get yourself out of the way and love others.

Living it

Where there is no love, pour love in, and you will draw love out.
– St. John of the Cross

Nothing Is Too Hard for God

"With man this is impossible, but with God all things are possible."

~ MATTHEW 19:26

Has a situation ever seemed hopeless to you, but then God steps in and things work out in a way better than you could have imagined? We may work ourselves silly trying to "fix things" when all we really need to do is step out of the way and let God work. Nothing is beyond His power.

Jesus made the statement in the above verse in reference to the fact that if it were up to humans, no one would get into heaven. But with God there is a way. Nothing is too hard for Him – nothing.

Living it

Ah, Sovereign LORD, You have made the heavens and the earth by Your great power and outstretched arm. Nothing is too hard for You.

– Jeremiah 32:17

God Cares

"If that is how God clothes the grass of the field, which is here today, and tomorrow is thrown into the fire, how much more will He clothe you – you of little faith!"

~ LUKE 12:28

Sometimes life is tough. Horrible things happen around the world: earthquakes, hurricanes, tsunamis, floods. Hard things also happen in your life; a loved one dies, a friend hurts you, a job is lost.

When life gets heavy, do you sometimes wonder if God even cares? Of course you know He does, even though He doesn't take away your problems. But look at this – He even dresses the fields. He won't leave you alone to go through hardship. Trust that He is with you regardless of how tough life is. Trust Him to bring you through and believe that He loves you, no matter what.

Living it

Keep trusting God. He is always in control even when your circumstances may seem out of control.

– Anonymous

Your Job!

"Go into all the world and preach the gospel to all creation."

~ MARK 16:15

Heads up – this isn't a suggestion. It's a command. You know the good news of Jesus' love. How will other people know about it if you don't tell them? OK, so you're not a preacher. Maybe you're not a teacher, either.

But you are a friend, a co-worker, a family member, and you can share Jesus' love by the way you live in front of others. You can answer their questions about faith or invite them to events where they will hear the gospel. Jesus said to make sure everyone has a chance to hear it. Use the talents He gave you and do all you can.

Living it

For all have sinned and fall short of the glory of God, and all are justified freely by His grace through the redemption that came by Christ Jesus.

– Romans 3:23-24

The Basics

"This is My command: Love each other."
~ JOHN 15:17

It's so basic – just love each other. But it's not always basic to do. Why is it so hard sometimes? Maybe it's because "self" gets in the way and your focus is on how circumstances affect you or whether you're being treated fairly. Sometimes it's because people have different beliefs, and, well let's face it, some people are difficult to love.

But just think – if everyone obeyed this basic command and gave others a second chance or the benefit of the doubt – as each of us wants for ourselves – then our world would be a lot more pleasant! May it begin today, with each of us.

Living it

We have committed the Golden Rule to memory; let us now commit it to life.
– Edward Markham

Forgiving Others

"If your brother or sister sins against you, rebuke them; and if they repent, forgive them. Even if they sin against you seven times in a day and seven times come back to you saying, 'I repent,' you must forgive them."

~ LUKE 17:3-4

When a friend apologizes it's important to forgive and then to forget. In fact, Jesus says to forgive over and over and over. Wow, that's hard if you feel you're being taken advantage of or lied to. It's OK to draw some boundaries, but be fair.

Remember that God forgives you over and over and over. So shouldn't you be willing to do the same? Set boundaries but be reasonable. Take your own ego out of the equation. Give others a second, third and fourth chance. After all, that's what love does.

Living it

Bear with each other and forgive one another if any of you has a grievance against someone. Forgive as the Lord forgave you.

– Colossians 3:13

Peacemakers!

"Blessed are the peacemakers, for they will be called children of God."

~ MATTHEW 5:9

A great deal of Jesus' teaching focuses on loving and helping others. He makes it clear that one element of that relates to being a peaceful person.

Peacemakers will be called sons of God, He says. The opposite of a peacemaker would be … what? A troublemaker? Someone who criticizes others, picks arguments, pits people against each other and just generally keeps things stirred up and anything but peaceful?

A peacemaker bridges over the differences that a troublemaker creates. A peacemaker shows love to others. Where do you fit in? Are you a peacemaker or a troublemaker?

Living it

Dear Father,

I want to be a peacemaker. I see how important this is to You. Forgive me for the times when I was the problem in a situation rather than the peaceful one. Help me, Father, to be more peaceful by trusting You with people and situations. In Jesus' name, Amen.

No Reason for Pride

"Those who exalt themselves will be humbled, and those who humble themselves will be exalted."

~ MATTHEW 23:12

There is a fine line between confidence and pride; between knowing who you are and what your gifts are ... yep, pride. What's the difference? It is the knowledge that who you are and whatever gifts or talents you possess has absolutely nothing to do with you. It all comes from God.

The reality is that you have nothing to brag about, so don't be proud; be humble. Don't push others down so that you can push yourself up. Don't make yourself more important than others and definitely not more important than God. Give all glory, honor and praise to Him.

Living it

A proud man is always looking down on things and people; and, of course, as long as you're looking down, you can't see something that's above you.

– C. S. Lewis

Need vs. Want

"Your Father knows what you need before you ask Him."
~ MATTHEW 6:8

These words are so very comforting. God knows what you need even before you ask Him! He anticipates your need because He loves you very much. He also knows the difference between what you *need* and what you *want*. He may not always give what you want, because He knows it isn't what you need. He can see the full picture of your life so He knows what you need in every situation and for every task.

Since He knows your needs, does that mean you don't have to ask Him? No, do ask … asking reminds you that you are trusting God.

Living it

Dear Father,
Help me remember this – You know what I need. Sometimes the line between what I need and what I want gets blurred. Help me remember that You know the important stuff and You will always take care of me.
In Jesus' name, Amen.

Revealing Light

"Everyone who does evil hates the light, and will not come into the light for fear that their deeds will be exposed."

~ JOHN 3:20

*T*hings are hidden in darkness, but when a light is turned on, all is revealed. So it makes sense that people who do dishonest, unkind or hurtful things to others would want to stay in darkness where no one can see what they are doing.

Jesus says that He is the Light of the world. People who do evil things would want to stay away from Him so their behavior would not be so obvious.

Are you in darkness or are you in the light? If you are in the light, remember that your actions and attitudes are revealed. Make sure they bring honor to God.

Living it

The LORD is my light and my salvation – whom shall I fear? The LORD is the stronghold of my life – of whom shall I be afraid?

– Psalm 27:1

Life-Giving Water!

"Everyone who drinks this water will be thirsty again, but whoever drinks the water I give them will never thirst. Indeed, the water I give them will become in them a spring of water welling up to eternal life."

~ JOHN 4:13-14

Jesus says that He offers everything you need. What does that mean? Well, pretty much everyone is born with a thirst to be loved and to know they matter to someone. They want meaning in their lives.

Some people try to quench this thirst by accumulating wealth. Some turn to alcohol or drugs. Those things might work for a while, but the only thing that will quench the thirst to be loved forever is Jesus. He lasts for eternity.

Living it

How does Jesus show His love for you?

How has your awareness of His love for you grown as you have known Him longer?

How does Jesus' love give meaning to your life?

Trust like a Child!

"Let the little children come to Me, and do not hinder them, for the kingdom of God belongs to such as these."

~ MARK 10:14

Why did Jesus say that God's kingdom belongs to children? Perhaps because children easily trust, and don't argue about every point or need to have things proven to them. As people grow up, they lose that child-like trust.

Some adults question everything and demand God's immediate action – therefore no trust is shown. Child-like faith is much more pleasing to God because it is a faith that just trusts Him. How are you doing at trusting God?

Living it

In what part of life do you have the most trouble with trust? Why is that area so difficult? How can you begin with one small act of trust so that you take small steps to grow your trust?

Real Love

"Love your enemies, do good to those who hate you, bless those who curse you, pray for those who mistreat you."
~ LUKE 6:27-28

Oh, come on. Love your enemies? Seriously? Does Jesus know what He is asking here? Of course He does. Let's face it – it's easy to love people who love you back and treat you well. Remember that Jesus said the second greatest commandment is to love your neighbor as yourself.

The real test of Christian love is loving people who are different from you, lie about you, cheat you, say mean things or just generally treat you badly. If you can love these people and pray for them, then you are truly showing Jesus' love.

Living it

Do I not destroy my enemies when I make them my friends?
– Abraham Lincoln

A good man is kinder to his enemy than bad men to his friends.
– Joseph Hall

February

God's Total Control

"Are not two sparrows sold for a penny? Yet not one of them will fall to the ground outside your Father's care."
~ Matthew 10:29

Sparrows are nothing special. They are common, ordinary birds that can be found pretty much everywhere. But even common sparrows are special to God. The message of Jesus' words here is that God knows what is happening in every bit of His creation; even little sparrows matter to Him.

If a plain, unspectacular bird can't fall from the sky without God deciding on that action, then you can believe that He is in control of everything in your life, too.

Living it

Dear Father,
I'm so glad You are in control of my life. I may not always act like I'm happy about that ... but I am. Thank You for guiding and blessing me. Thank You for taking care of me. Please help me to learn to trust You even more completely.
In Jesus' name, Amen.

You Can't Out-Give God

"Give, and it will be given to you. A good measure, pressed down, shaken together and running over, will be poured into your lap."

~ LUKE 6:38

You simply cannot out-give God. The more you give to Him by doing His work and serving His people, the more He will give you.

If you have ever baked using brown sugar as an ingredient, you know that you put brown sugar in the measuring cup, press it down and add more, press it down again and add more. It's amazing how much sugar you can get in a measuring cup. That's how God's blessings are to those who are generous.

When you give, God gives, too. He just gives and gives and gives. You cannot imagine how much He will give you through His blessings and His love!

Living it

Sometimes prayer lists get so long – filled with the heart-felt needs of people you care about. But it's always good to stop and count your blessings. Make a list of the top five ways God has blessed your life.

Let Your Light Shine!

"Let your light shine before others, that they may see your good deeds and glorify your Father in heaven."
~ Matthew 5:16

When you ask Jesus to be your Savior, His light begins to shine through you because He is the Light of the world. Jesus said to let your light shine! What does that look like? You show love to others – even people who aren't your friends. You lift others up and help them succeed. You put others before yourself. The goal is not praise for how great you are.

When people know that you are a Christian and they see the light of your love and kind deeds shining, then they give credit for it to God. Your light is a witness to God!

Living it

God is light; in Him there is no darkness at all. If we claim to have fellowship with Him and yet walk in the darkness, we lie and do not live out the truth. But if we walk in the light, as He is in the light, we have fellowship with one another, and the blood of Jesus, His Son, purifies us from all sin.
– 1 John 1:5-7

Believing God's Word

"Some people are like seed along the path, where the word is sown. As soon as they hear it, Satan comes and takes away the word that was sown in them."

~ MARK 4:15

Some people hear the truth of God's Word but don't accept it in their heart. Just hearing God's Word is not enough. It's a good starting point, because you have to hear before you can believe, but you can't stop with hearing. You must hear, accept and believe, then put His Word into action in your life.

When you keep God at a distance, it gives Satan a chance to sneak in and steal His truth away, keeping your faith from taking root and growing.

Living it

Come near to God and He will come near to you.

– James 4:8

Harvest Workers

"The harvest is plentiful, but the workers are few. Ask the Lord of the harvest, therefore, to send out workers into His harvest field."

~ LUKE 10:2

God's plan is for everyone in the world to have a chance to hear about His love. Many people will believe and accept Jesus as Savior if they just get the opportunity to hear about Him. Here's the challenge: Do your part in sharing the message of His love with others in the world.

You know that missionaries leave their family and home to travel the world, telling people of God's love. Of course, some people give money to help those who go. Some people pray for the missionaries. Some people minister in their own neighborhoods. Do what God calls you to do, wherever and whatever it may be.

Living it

Dear Father,

I really care about all people having the opportunity to hear about Your love. I'm just not sure what I should or could do to help with that. Show me, Lord, how to be a part of Your work in this world.

In Jesus' name, Amen.

Loving Your Brothers and Sisters

"By this everyone will know that you are My disciples, if you love one another."

~ JOHN 13:35

*D*oes Jesus mean that His disciples never lose their cool, never argue with others, always agree with everything that comes their way? Probably not … He knows we're human and relationships can be complicated and challenging. So what does He mean?

Loving someone means treating them with respect, even when you disagree. If the members of Jesus' family can't get along with each other, why would others want to be a part of it? We should be bound together by our love for Jesus and our love for one another.

Don't let little things come between you and other Christians; if they do, resolve them quickly and with honor and respect.

Living it

The days are too short even for love; how can there be enough time for quarreling?

– Margaret Gatty

Worship Only God

"Away from Me, Satan! For it is written: 'Worship the Lord your God, and serve Him only.'"
~ Matthew 4:10

O K, be honest, life is hard sometimes. Broken relationships, lost jobs, health problems. So if someone offered to make everything better; offered you the world, and all you had to do was worship this person … would you do it? Satan tried this and Jesus told him to get lost. He replied that Scripture says to worship God and serve only Him.

There are two key things to notice here. One is that Jesus knew what was written in Scripture. Knowing Scripture is important. The second thing is that Jesus declared that God should be more important than anything else. Worship only God!

Living it

Your word is a lamp for my feet, a light for my path.
– Psalm 119:105

Sharing the Wealth

"It is easier for a camel to go through the eye of a needle than for a rich person to enter the Kingdom of God."

~ MARK 10:25 NLT

Sometimes people want the right things, but they want to take a shortcut to get them. A rich young man wanted to know what he had to do to be saved – he wanted the right thing. Jesus told him to give away all his wealth, but the rich man couldn't do that. He was looking for an easy way to salvation.

For some people money becomes more important than God. Don't let money become the focus of your life. Wealth won't get you to heaven … and won't buy you happiness. Only knowing Jesus will bring true happiness in a relationship with Him.

Living it

We make a living by what we get, but we make a life by what we give.

– Winston Churchill

Fishing for Men

"Don't be afraid; from now on you will fish for people."
~ LUKE 5:10

When Jesus called His disciples to follow Him, He didn't want just their devotion. He had work for them to do. Several of them were fishermen when He called them. They left their work and followed Him immediately.

Jesus explained the work He had for them to do in ways they would understand. They would be catching men, in other words, winning people to faith in Him. This is such important work and it continues to this day for each of Jesus' followers – win people to faith in Him.

Living it

Lost people matter to God, and so they must matter to us.
– Keith Wright

Actions That Match Your Words

"If you love Me, obey My commandments."

~ JOHN 14:15 NLT

What's your answer to the pointed question, "Do you love God?" More than likely you will say, "Yes, of course I love Him." That's good, but take some time and think about this question: Do your actions bear that out?

You may say that you love God. You may even feel you mean it. But the real proof that you love Him is evident by your obedience to Jesus' teachings. That means things like how you treat other people; whether you're self-involved and self-centered. Are you honest and fair; are you sacrificial in your dealings with others?

OK, honesty time … you're the only one who can answer this question: Do you follow Jesus' teachings to the best of your ability and then ask Him to help you obey more?

Living it

Have you noticed how much praying for revival has been going on of late – and how little revival has resulted? I believe the problem is that we have been trying to substitute praying for obeying, and it simply will not work.

– A. W. Tozer

What's Your Motivation?

"When you give to the needy, do not announce it with trumpets, as the hypocrites do in the synagogues and on the streets, to be honored by others. Truly I tell you, they have received their reward in full."

~ MATTHEW 6:2

There is a popular Christian chorus that has a line in it which asks God to "break my heart for what breaks Yours." When God lays something on your heart that motivates you to action, whether it be by giving or doing for someone else, that's a blessed thing. But, when you answer God's call on your life – do so humbly. Don't call attention to yourself or your sacrifices.

Your service to God is between you and Him. Don't look for the praise or adoration of others.

Living it

Do you wish to be great? Then begin by being. Do you desire to construct a vast and lofty fabric? Think first about the foundations of humility. The higher your structure is to be, the deeper must be its foundation.

– St. Augustine

You Are Very Special

"What do you think? If a man owns a hundred sheep, and one of them wanders away, will he not leave the ninety-nine on the hills and go to look for the one that wandered off?"

~ MATTHEW 18:12

Do you ever feel as if you're lost in the crowd? After all, God has so many people to take care of and so many crises to handle. Do you wonder if He has the time to take care of your issues? Or maybe, once in a while you feel like you are at the back of the crowd, waving your hand in the air to get His attention.

How precious then, are these words from Jesus that reassure you that every person is important to God. Whether it is when a person comes to faith or when a child is struggling, He cares enough to leave the crowd so that He can look for and rescue the one. You are special. Very special.

Living it

Dear Father,

I needed this today. I do feel lost in the crowd sometimes, but I long to know ... and believe that You love me completely. Thank You for the reminder that You do.

In Jesus' name, Amen.

The Growing Kingdom of God

"What is the kingdom of God like? What shall I compare it to? It is like a mustard seed, which a man took and planted in his garden. It grew and became a tree, and the birds perched in its branches."

~ LUKE 13:18-19

Nothing starts out full-grown. People, organizations, ministries, relationships … each thing has a starting point from which it grows. God's kingdom on earth started small as a mustard seed, but has grown fantastically and is continuing to grow.

You have a part in making that growth happen. It's pretty cool to be a part of something so amazing. So, at times when you feel alone, remember you're a part of a big kingdom! It's a family!

Living it

Dear Father,

I'm so blessed to be a part of Your family … to feel that I belong to something so amazing and so real. God, I want to tell others about Your kingdom. Show me how to do that and give me the courage to share.

In Jesus' name, Amen.

Be Careful of Your Influence

"If anyone causes one of these little ones – those who believe in Me – to stumble, it would be better for them if a large millstone were hung around their neck and they were thrown into the sea."

~ MARK 9:42

Children matter to Jesus. He warns people to think about how they affect and influence children. The truth is that sin is serious business, even though we don't talk about it much. How do you cause someone else to sin? Sometimes it is through your example.

People, especially children, watch to see how Christians act and react, the words they use, the tone of their voice … and they could be led to behave in ways that do not honor God because of the example they see. Big responsibility, huh? Asking God for help and awareness is a good idea.

Living it

Dear Father,
I needed this reminder about sin. I confess to You that I don't think about my sin very often. Please open my eyes to the ways I am a poor influence on others. I want people to see You when they see me. Help me, Lord.

In Jesus' name, Amen.

No Fence Sitting

"Whoever believes in Him is not condemned, but whoever does not believe stands condemned already because they have not believed in the name of God's one and only Son."
~ JOHN 3:18

You either believe in Jesus or you don't. It is not possible to sort of believe anymore than it is possible to sort of be pregnant. You can't ride the fence on this truth. Believing in Jesus is the only way to heaven.

To be saved you must believe that Jesus is God's only Son who was free from sin but came to earth and died for your sins so that your heart could be cleansed. God raised Him back to life and He is waiting to spend forever with you in heaven. Have you believed? Truly and completely?

Living it

When is your "spiritual birthday?" When did you ask Jesus to be your Savior? Do you remember the experience? Has your faith grown stronger since that day? Have you followed Jesus truly and completely?

Comfort from Jesus

"Blessed are those who mourn, for they will be comforted."

~ Matthew 5:4

Mourning is painful. Mourning is draining. Mourning is part of life because loss is a part of life. Jesus promises that those who are mourning losses will be comforted if they turn to Him. Think about it … Jesus cares when you are mourning. He cares that you hurt. Jesus loves you so very much that He will surround you with His love to comfort you when you are grieving.

You will learn more about Jesus, and your relationship with Him will grow stronger if you lean on Him when you hurt. Trust Him. Lean on Him. Let Him be your comfort.

Living it

He will wipe every tear from their eyes. There will be no more death or mourning or crying or pain, for the old order of things has passed away.

– Revelation 21:4

Prayers from the Heart

"When you pray, do not be like the hypocrites, for they love to pray standing in the synagogues and on the street corners to be seen by others. Truly I tell you, they have received their reward in full."

~ MATTHEW 6:5

*P*rayer is the opportunity to communicate with God – to tell Him what you're thinking, what you care about, what you would like Him to do. Prayer also offers the opportunity to praise, honor and worship God.

Prayer should come from the heart. Trying to impress God with fancy words will not fool Him. Showy prayers will draw attention to you, but they won't honor God. Just talk to Him … from your heart.

Living it

To be a Christian without prayer is no more possible than to be alive without breathing.

– Martin Luther King, Jr.

Use It for God

"I tell you that to everyone who has, more will be given, but as for the one who has nothing, even what they have will be taken away."

~ LUKE 19:26

God has given every person certain abilities and gifts. Those things are His investment in you and are to be used to grow His kingdom. If you don't use them … you'll lose them.

Each talent, skill and ability you have is a gift from Him and He wants you to use each one to honor Him and share His love with others. If you're not sure what gifts He gave you – ask Him to make them clear and then pray for opportunities to serve Him with your talents and gifts.

Living it

Now you are the body of Christ, and each one of you is a part of it.

– 1 Corinthians 12:27

What Are You Working For?

"Do not work for food that spoils, but for food that endures to eternal life, which the Son of Man will give you. For on Him God the Father has placed His seal of approval."
~ JOHN 6:27

What are you working for? What's your focus in life? You may answer that God is most important to you. That is how it should be. However, look back over your day or week and notice where are you putting your time and energy.

Jesus encouraged people to put their energy and focus on serving God, because that is an investment in eternity. Know God, read His Word, serve and obey Him. That will give you food that lasts forever.

Living it

Do you really want to see where your time goes? Keep a spreadsheet for a week to record what you do every minute of the day. Are you surprised at where your time goes? Do you need to make adjustments in your priorities?

Life Model

"I have set you an example that you should do as I have done for you."

~ John 13:15

Jesus gave an example of how to live a life that honors God. His own life is that model. His example is honoring God, caring for others and offering humble service.

What's even more amazing is that He made the statement above right after He washed His disciples' feet. That was a humbling job to do for others; in fact it was a job normally done by a servant. By doing so, Jesus showed His followers how to serve others in humility. Don't let your own ego or pride get in the way of serving God or others.

Living it

In His life, Christ is an example, showing us how to live.

– Martin Luther

An Amazing Gift

"I will ask the Father, and He will give you another Advocate to help you and be with you forever – the Spirit of truth."
~ JOHN 14:16-17

Jesus had to leave the earth. He made that departure easier for His followers to take by promising to send the Holy Spirit. What a gift! Since the Spirit lives in our hearts, we know that God is always with us. He helps us to know right from wrong and guides us to recognize what is true and honest.

The Holy Spirit helps us serve God and reminds us how much God loves us because He never leaves us alone. The Spirit even prays for us when we can't find the words to pray. What an amazing gift.

Living it

May Your unfailing love be my comfort, according to Your promise to Your servant.
– Psalm 119:76

Holding Nothing Back

"They all gave out of their wealth; but she, out of her poverty, put in everything – all she had to live on."

~ MARK 12:44

You may know the story of the widow who gave two small coins in the temple. Two coins that were barely worth a penny. Doesn't seem like much, does it? Especially when you consider that wealthier people in the temple were giving much larger offerings.

Jesus honored this woman's gift because she gave all she had. She held nothing back from God. The rich man's gift was larger, but it didn't really cost him much. He had so much money that the gift was extra money to him. Jesus looks at the heart of the giver and how much she holds back for herself compared with how much she is willing to give to others. Will you give Jesus everything?

Living it

There are three kinds of givers – the flint, the sponge and the honeycomb. To get anything out of a flint you must hammer it. And then you get only chips and sparks. To get water out of a sponge you must squeeze it, and the more you use pressure, the more you will get. But the honeycomb just overflows with its own sweetness. Which kind of giver are you?

– Anonymous

Most Important Rules

"I tell you that unless your righteousness surpasses that of the Pharisees and the teachers of the law, you will certainly not enter the kingdom of heaven."

~ MATTHEW 5:20

Jesus didn't mince words, did He? He knew that the Pharisees and teachers of the law knew the Scriptures and even taught them to the people. They should have been the most righteous people as examples of God's servants.

But they weren't. They were filled with pride so they thought they knew more than the Scriptures. Their biggest mistake was that they got so caught up in rules that they forgot what God said was most important … loving others! Righteousness is shown by love. Don't get caught up in rules or prideful living.

Living it

Dear Father,

I don't want to be like that. I know that I do get caught up in rules sometimes, but only because rules make me comfortable. But, God, I don't want to lose relationships or the focus on loving others. Help me make love and compassion my priority.

In Jesus' name, Amen.

Finding Your Way

"Enter through the narrow gate. For wide is the gate and broad is the road that leads to destruction, and many enter through it."

~ MATTHEW 7:13

When you chose to follow Christ, you were given the Holy Spirit to help you, teach you, guide you and protect you. But, even with His presence, it isn't always easy to live for God. That's OK because something that is worthwhile is never easy.

Some people choose the easy way through life. They think that the wide path looks like the best way because it seems to have fewer rules and gives more control over your own life. However, the narrow way is the one that leads to God and actually offers more freedom because you have His protection and wisdom. It keeps you focused on loving and obeying Him as you love and serve others.

Living it

Now the Lord is the Spirit, and where the Spirit of the Lord is, there is freedom.

– 2 Corinthians 3:17

Dependency

"Ask and it will be given to you; seek and you will find; knock
and the door will be opened to you."
~ MATTHEW 7:7

Society says that to be a successful woman you must be
strong and independent. There's nothing wrong with
that, unless a strong woman becomes so independent
that she finds it difficult to ask for help when she needs
it … even from God.

Are you a strong, independent woman who struggles
to ask for help? You do know that God wants to help you.
He wants to know what weighs on your heart and what
keeps you awake at night. Let go of your stubbornness
and tell Him what your heart yearns for. Be persistent
and honest. That's what an honest relationship is built
on. Ask. Seek. Knock and you will find.

Living it

Don't pray when you feel like it. Have an appointment with
the Lord and keep it. A man is powerful on his knees.
– Corrie ten Boom

Source of Life

"I am the true vine, and My Father is the gardener."

~ JOHN 15:1

*I*f you've done any gardening, you'll know the importance of a strong root system and healthy vines or stems to grow lovely flowers or good fruit. The vine is the transit system for nutrition. Jesus said that He is the vine and as the vine Jesus brings nutrition to His children.

A relationship with Him brings the power and courage to grow in strength. Jesus is your connection to God, the Father of all things. Stay close to Jesus, because that relationship is the source of your life.

Living it

Dear Father,
I understand the necessity to stay close to You in order to get the nutrition I need to grow. I need help with discipline to have a daily quiet time with You and to make time to be still before You. I want those things. Help me to do them.

In Jesus' name, Amen.

You Matter

"In the same way, I tell you, there is rejoicing in the presence of the angels of God over one sinner who repents."
~ LUKE 15:10

You matter to God. The choices you make matter to Him. In this crazy, over-committed, demanding life there may be times when you wonder if anyone is paying attention to you. God is. He drops everything to celebrate when you trust Him. If He does that, it just makes sense that He also celebrates your victories and empathizes with your hurts. He cares.

Read this verse again. Jesus made this statement after talking about how a woman looked everywhere to find one lost coin. When she found it all her friends came and celebrated with her! Let it be a reminder that Jesus loves *you*.

Living it

Though our feelings come and go, God's love for us does not.
– C. S. Lewis

Talk Is Cheap

"These people honor Me with their lips, but their hearts are far from Me."

~ MARK 7:6

Blah, blah, blah. So you know all the "Christian" words to say. Good for you … or a big "so what?" The truth is that just saying Christian words doesn't mean you are honoring or serving God. Oh, sure, it may look like you are and you may be fooling others and even yourself. But you're not fooling God.

What's happening in your heart is the true measurement of your relationship with Him. Don't bother with the fancy words if your heart is full of selfishness or evil. Ask Him to clean up your heart and then honest words will come naturally.

Living it

Dear Father,
Please search my heart and see if my words match what's in my heart. I want my worship for You to be honest. Teach me, Lord, to know You better and follow You more closely.

In Jesus' name, Amen.

Comfort

"My Father is always at His work to this very day, and I too am working."
~ JOHN 5:17

It's an amazing comfort to know that God is never on vacation. He never takes a day off. He always knows what's happening. Jesus says that He and His Father are working together.

You know that He loves you so you can know that He's paying attention to your life with all its ups and downs. Believe that – even when you can't seem to find Him or sense His presence; just trust in His love and care. You never have to worry about whether God knows what you're dealing with. He does … and He's working on it.

Living it

God demonstrates His own love for us in this: While we were still sinners, Christ died for us.
– Romans 5:8

March

No Passes on Tough Love

"If you love those who love you, what credit is that to you? Even sinners love those who love them."
~ LUKE 6:32

Unfortunately some Christians have developed a reputation for being judgmental and critical. According to this verse, Jesus doesn't approve of that kind of spirit. Jesus didn't give any passes regarding those who are hard to love. After all, it's easy to love those who agree with your opinions; those who like the same things you enjoy; those who are a lot like you.

But what about people who aren't loveable? What about those who have different political or religious views? Do you have to love them? Yep! How do you do it? Let God love them through you. He'll do the hard work, you just let Him.

Living it

We love because He first loved us.
– 1 John 4:19

True Fruit

"By their fruit you will recognize them. Do people pick grapes from thornbushes, or figs from thistles?"

~ Matthew 7:16

Jesus didn't mince words. He made it clear that if you are living for Him, your life will show it. Your behavior speaks loudly as to what you truly believe. A woman who is serving and obeying God will soon have fruit in her life.

What is fruit? A growing love for Jesus and for other people. A desire to witness for Him and share His love with others. A willingness to use the gifts and talents God has given to grow His kingdom. A woman can claim to be following Christ, but if there's no fruit in her life then her words are empty.

Living it

The highest form of worship is the worship of unselfish Christian service.

– Billy Graham

Evidence from Inside

"What comes out of a person is what defiles them."
~ Mark 7:20

Perhaps you have been the recipient of a spate of ugly words spewed at you from a friend. Or, maybe you have witnessed some unkind behavior toward another person. These experiences are especially hard when they come from a Christian sister who claims to have a relationship with God. It's yet another example of a good appearance on the outside … but the real heart of a person shows in actions and words.

Make sure your heart is clean. Ask Jesus' help in getting rid of the things that make it unclean so that your words and actions reveal His love to all around you.

Living it

Review your interactions with others over the last week. Have your words and actions shown the love of Jesus to others? Or do you see that your heart might need some cleansing?

A New Command

"A new command I give you: Love one another. As I have loved you, so you must love one another."

~ JOHN 13:34

L ove one another. It should be simple, but it isn't always. Jesus says to love. Just love. But things, stuff, people, the self get in the way of that love. What's your particular roadblock to loving others? Sadly, more often than not the problem with loving others is you.

It's easy to become self-focused and locked in on how every situation, every relationship, every *thing* affects you.

Real love for others means putting the self aside and sacrificially loving others by being concerned for their well-being and growth. We do this by giving time, energy and help to others. Love as Jesus loves.

Living it

God sends no one away empty except those who are full of themselves.

– Dwight L. Moody

Belief Instead of Fear

"Don't be afraid; just believe."

~ MARK 5:36

Fear is paralyzing to faith. It's impossible for fear and faith to occupy the same heart. Jesus says, "No problem ... just believe. Just trust." It's easy to say, but not always easy to do. If fear is something you struggle with you may need to learn to trust with baby steps of believing. But remember that Jesus spoke these words to a father who had just been told that his daughter was dead.

Imagine hearing Jesus say don't be afraid when someone you dearly love has just died? But the father did trust Jesus and his trust was rewarded. There's no situation Jesus can't handle ... none.

Living it

Dear Father,

Sometimes I feel paralyzed by my fears. It's humbling to realize that my fear means I don't trust You. Help me to trust more and fear less, Father. Help me to understand the depth of Your love for me. Thank You. Thank You for Your love and care.

In Jesus' name, Amen.

Jesus Meets Your Needs

"Very truly I tell you, you are looking for Me, not because you saw signs I performed but because you ate the loaves and had your fill."

~ JOHN 6:26

Why did people constantly surround Jesus? He knew why. People wanted to be close to Him for what they could get from Him … not for what they could learn from Him. He came to teach, inspire and encourage people to turn to God.

The people got caught up in the miracles He performed, of healing and feeding and raising dead people back to life. That's what they wanted. They wanted the miraculous instead of the constant love and they didn't want to hear what He taught. Hmm, it's easy to criticize these people.

Why do you want to be close to Jesus? What do you want from Him?

Living it

Do you want a close, personal relationship with Jesus? Or do you want the "stuff" that knowing Him brings? If you could have His blessings without the relationship, would that be enough? The relationship, filled with His love and care, is more wonderful than any of the "extras."

Resting in Jesus

"Come to Me, all you who are weary and burdened, and I will give you rest."
~ MATTHEW 11:28

Tired. Many women describe themselves as tired or even go beyond that to weary. Perhaps you are one of these women and perhaps you aren't just physically weary, either. This crazy, fast-paced, demanding world you live in wears you out emotionally and even spiritually sometimes.

Jesus says the answer to that weariness is to lean on Him. Trust Him to take care of you and those you love. Trust Him to take care of whatever makes you weary. He will give the necessary strength and encouragement to keep on going.

Living it

Trust in the LORD with all your heart and lean not on your own understanding; in all your ways submit to Him, and He will make your paths straight.
– Proverbs 3:5-6

Remember!

"This is My body given for you; do this in remembrance of Me."

~ LUKE 22:19

Jesus gave this instruction to His disciples at the Last Supper – the meal they shared before He was arrested. He knew the end of His earthly life was near so He told them that when they ate the bread and drank the wine that they should remember Him. He didn't mean they should just remember their friend named Jesus. They should remember what He did for them (and us) by His death and resurrection. He gave the ultimate gift of love.

Don't approach communion lightly or out of habit. Remember that eternal life with Jesus is possible because of the sacrificial gift He gave.

Living it

Dear Father,
Thank You for Jesus' sacrifice for me. I will never take it lightly. Lord, I pray for an open heart to be aware of my shortcomings so that each time I take communion I am reminded of Jesus' gift.

In Jesus' name, Amen.

Wholehearted Service

"No one can serve two masters. Either you will hate the one and love the other, or you will be devoted to the one and despise the other. You cannot serve both God and money."
~ MATTHEW 6:24

*T*his is where the rubber meets the road. You're either serving God or you're not – doesn't matter what you say you're doing. Your words and actions will eventually reveal who or what you are truly serving.

Following God halfheartedly is not following God at all. If He doesn't have all the devotion of your heart, then whatever is claiming the other part of it will eventually push God out of the way. Where's your heart?

Living it

Be very careful to keep the commandment and the law that Moses the servant of the LORD gave you: to love the LORD your God, to walk in obedience to Him, to keep His commands, to hold fast to Him and to serve Him with all your heart and with all your soul.
– Joshua 22:5

Honest Belief

"Everything is possible for one who believes."

~ MARK 9:23

*D*o you believe this? Do you trust Jesus enough to believe that everything is possible? This deep belief and trust is not simple, but the truth of this statement is very exciting!

Jesus made this statement to a father who wanted help for his son. The father wanted Jesus' help, so he asked Jesus to help him believe. He knew his faith wasn't strong enough, but that Jesus could help it grow! Believe, and if you can't … ask Jesus to help you. There's always room for faith to grow.

Living it

I believe in the sun even if it isn't shining. I believe in love even when I am alone. I believe in God even when He is silent.

– Anonymous

Follow the Leader

"Go and do likewise."
~ LUKE 10:37

Pretty much everyone loves a good story and Jesus often taught by telling stories. One of His stories was about the Good Samaritan. You know the story: a man is beaten up by robbers. Two different men pass by the victim – church men – but they don't help him. A third man comes by, a Samaritan, an enemy of the Jews. But this Good Samaritan stops to help the hurt man.

Jesus finished the story by asking which of the three men was a neighbor to the hurt man. The answer was of course the third man. Jesus said, "Go and do likewise"! What's the lesson? Don't just help your friends. Help *anyone* who needs assistance.

Living it

Act as if what you do makes a difference. It does.
– William James

God's Love

"Even the very hairs of your head are all numbered. So don't be afraid; you are worth more than many sparrows."

~ MATTHEW 10:30-31

*D*o you understand how very much God loves you? Jesus knows everything about you. He knows everything that happens to you. Absolutely nothing surprises Him. Look at the world around you. God takes care of it. You are more important to Him than any animals or birds or trees. He even knows how many hairs there are on your head!

God knows every detail of your life. So, no matter what you're struggling with; no matter how confused you may be, rest in Him. Trust Him. Love Him.

Living it

Dear Father,
Thank You for Your love. There are times when I'm completely overwhelmed by Your love. There are also times, when I'm struggling, that I make myself stop and count the ways You show Your love for me. Regardless, I always believe it's there. I'm so grateful.

In Jesus' name, Amen.

Shallow-Root Christians

"Others, like seed sown on rocky places, hear the word and at once receive it with joy. But since they have no root, they last only a short time. When trouble or persecution comes because of the word, they quickly fall away."
~ MARK 4:16-17

Some people hear the news of God's love, accept it and get really excited about it. But at the first sign of trouble or disappointment, they fall away. Why? Because they haven't developed roots – depth to their faith. There are ups and downs in life – even for Christians.

A woman who reads her Bible gets to know God better and better learns that she can trust Him. Accordingly, the roots of her faith grow stronger. Then when problems come she has the necessary faith to keep trusting God. But, if she doesn't invest in knowing God better, she has no roots to keep her strong in her faith. Are you investing in your faith?

Living it

God is God. Because He is God, He is worthy of my trust and obedience. I will find rest nowhere but in His holy will, a will that is unspeakably beyond my largest notions of what He is up to.
– Elisabeth Elliot

Loving Everyone

"If you do good to those who are good to you, what credit is that to you? Even sinners do that."

~ Luke 6:33

Jesus had an amazing way of cutting to the heart of the matter. He told it like it was – helping only people who can do something for you, He said, is nothing to be proud of. It's not obeying Jesus. It's using people for your own purposes. Any woman can do that; even if she doesn't know Jesus.

Real evidence that a person's heart wants to serve Jesus is when she can serve God and love Him by loving *all* people, not just her friends. That is the goal Jesus has for you!

Living it

Be kind and compassionate to one another, forgiving each other, just as in Christ God forgave you.

– Ephesians 4:32

Happiness from Knowing Jesus

"Anyone who drinks this water will soon become thirsty again. But those who drink the water I give will never be thirsty again. It becomes a fresh, bubbling spring within them, giving them eternal life."

~ JOHN 4:13-14 NLT

If you are looking for fulfillment in places other than Jesus you are just wasting your time. You can focus your time and energy on money, job success, power … whatever is important to you and for a while you might be on top of the world.

But the fulfillment of those things will wear thin after a while. There will be a place deep in your soul that remains unsatisfied. Nothing will permanently satisfy you like a strong, intimate relationship with Jesus. That's the only thing that lasts forever.

Living it

Dear Father,

I long for that water that quenches all thirst. Father, help me to keep my focus on You. It's so easy to let other things take over that focus. It's a daily decision to put You first and live for You. That's my choice. Help me stick to it. Thanks.

In Jesus' name, Amen

By the Book

"Let it be so now; it is proper for us to do this to fulfill all righteousness."

~ MATTHEW 3:15

Jesus had just asked John the Baptist to baptize Him but John resisted. John said that Jesus should baptize him instead. But, Jesus always paid attention to what was right. He didn't want anyone to be able to say that He wasn't truly the Messiah, because things didn't happen the way the prophets had said they would.

He wanted to do things by the book. Hmm, something to think about … if Jesus lived by the book (the Bible) then so should you.

Living it

Oh, how I love Your law! I meditate on it all day long. Your commands are always with me and make me wiser than my enemies. I have kept my feet from every evil path so that I might obey Your word.

– Psalm 119:97-98, 101

Jesus Is the Strongest!

"I have told you these things, so that in Me you may have peace. In this world you will have trouble. But take heart! I have overcome the world."

~ JOHN 16:33

*D*o you find it comforting to know that Jesus understood that life is full of all kinds of trouble? Nothing surprises Him. Even people who follow Jesus will have trouble, but He promised to give peace to those who follow him.

Does that mean He will take the troubles away? No, but He promised to be with you as you go through them. He gives strength and guidance to get through hard times. Turn to Jesus. Always turn to Him.

Living it

Dear Father,

I love that the Scriptures teach me that You are always with me – no matter what. Even if I can't see Your hand working, I can trust Your promise to guide, protect and love. I'm so grateful for that promise. I'm so blessed. Thank You.

In Jesus' name, Amen.

Jesus Sees the Truth

"All the nations will be gathered before Him, and He will separate the people one from another as a shepherd separates the sheep from the goats."

~ MATTHEW 25:32-33

Some people say that a loving God would never keep a person out of heaven. But that goes against what Scripture teaches. God gives everyone a chance to follow Him. But, choosing not to will have consequences. Every person will one day stand before God to answer for her decision as to whether or not she accepted Jesus as Savior.

People who have spent their lives only pretending to be Christians when it was convenient will find out that they have not fooled God. He will separate the believers from the unbelievers. Remember that God does not look at a person's activities. He looks at their hearts and sees the truth of what they believe.

Living it

Aim at heaven and you will get earth thrown in. Aim at earth and you will get neither.

– C. S. Lewis

Be Careful What You Think

"Why do you entertain evil thoughts in your hearts?"
~ MATTHEW 9:4

What does it mean to entertain evil thoughts? It means allowing your mind and heart to focus on things that are not honorable to God. It means you choose to think about things that pull you away from God; things that are immoral, things that destroy other people, things that are unkind. Sinful thoughts lead to sinful actions.

The Bible tells us to guard our hearts because Satan gets into our lives through hearts that aren't guarded. Choose to keep your heart focused on God, His love for you and the truths of the Bible. Then there will be no room for evil thoughts.

Living it

Above all else, guard your heart, for everything you do flows from it.
– Proverbs 4:23

Mercy Is as Mercy Does

"Be merciful, just as your Father is merciful."

~ LUKE 6:36

Mercy is one of those words that we only use when talking about Christian things. So, what is mercy? It's forgiveness that isn't deserved. It's kindness and compassion. God treats each of His children with mercy by His forgiveness and compassion, even though it isn't deserved. Jesus teaches you to treat others that way, too.

Since you are shown mercy, pass that along to others by your attitude and actions. Your Father (isn't it cool to know that God is your Father?) wants you to do so.

Living it

How can you show mercy today? Are there places and persons in your life where you've been harboring a bad attitude? Are there people you should forgive? Are there situations you need to accept? Perhaps you should ask God's help with showing mercy.

Serving by Caring

"Take care of My sheep."
~ John 21:16

Remember that Peter once told people he didn't even know Jesus (well, actually, he said that three times). But later, when that was all behind him, Jesus wanted to know how Peter really felt, so He asked Peter three times if he really loved Jesus. Of course Peter answered yes each time. After each answer, Jesus told him something – this time it was, "Feed My sheep."

Loving Jesus is more than just saying words; when you love Him, you serve Him, and that means taking action to help others. Jesus wants His followers to show His love to others by the way they live their lives.

Living it

Dear Father,
Sometimes loving others isn't easy … at least for me. Will You show me ways to love others – especially those who aren't especially loveable? I know You want me to "take care of Your sheep" just as You told Peter. I want to obey … please help me.
In Jesus' name, Amen.

For or Against

"Whoever is not with Me is against Me, and whoever does not gather with Me scatters."

~ Matthew 12:30

Remember the saying "Not to decide is to decide"? It's true. Once you hear about Jesus' love, then it's your choice to accept Jesus or not. Saying, "I'll decide later" is actually deciding not to accept Him. Or claiming you're with Jesus this day … but tomorrow something else is more important … well, you can't go back and forth.

Declaring Jesus by your words, but living a life that proves the words are empty, means you're not with Him. So, if you aren't for Jesus then you're against Him … not a good place to be.

Living it

When a brave man takes a stand, the spines of others are often stiffened.

– Billy Graham

Family Ties

"Whoever does God's will is my brother and sister and mother."
~ MARK 3:35

Family relationships are often the closest relationships on earth and are a visual of our place in God's own family. One of the joys of family is that members can honestly be themselves with one other. They love each other and support one another even if they don't always like each other.

Being a member of God's family is possible because Jesus came, lived and died for our sins and then rose again to life. Anyone can become a member of His family and that means you can be honest with Him – be real. What freedom, what joy. Accept Him, obey Him, serve Him. Be real with Him.

Living it

Dear Father,
I love that I can call You Father. I love that You love me that much. I'm so blessed to be a member of Your family. Thank You for loving me that much.
In Jesus' name, Amen.

The Importance of Scripture

"It is said: 'Do not put the Lord your God to the test.'"

~ LUKE 4:12

*D*o you put God to the test with prayers like, "God, show me Your love by doing this or that?" Whew. It's tempting when your heart is yearning for something to happen. Jesus understands temptation. In fact, He faced temptation when He was more tired and hungry that you can ever imagine.

When you have troubles, the evil one will whisper that God doesn't care. But it's not true. He does love you, enough to die for you. You don't need to test Him. He shows His love all the time. Yes, it's hard to be patient while waiting for His answers, but remember His love. Trust, don't test.

Living it

When tempted, no one should say, "God is tempting me." For God cannot be tempted by evil, nor does He tempt anyone; but each person is tempted when they are dragged away by their own evil desire and enticed. Then, after desire has conceived, it gives birth to sin; and sin, when it is full-grown, gives birth to death.

– James 1:13-15

The Best Example

"Now that I, your Lord and Teacher, have washed your feet, you also should wash one another's feet."

~ JOHN 13:14

Some people are easy to serve. Some people are difficult to serve. And, let's be honest; there may be times when you feel a bit too important to serve in the ways that are needed.

When it means getting down and dirty in distasteful jobs or working in heat and humidity – and no one even knows what you're doing! That's when it's important to remember this example – the Son of God doing a servant's job by washing His friends' dirty feet.

Jesus gave a beautiful example of a servant's heart that serves in basic, necessary, unglamorous ways. Go and do the same.

Living it

It is easy to love the people far away. It is not always easy to love those close to us. It is easier to give a cup of rice to relieve hunger than to relieve the loneliness and pain of someone unloved in our own home. Bring love into your home for this is where our love for each other must start.

– Mother Teresa

Honest Belief

"If you believe, you will receive whatever you ask for in prayer."

~ Matthew 21:22

So … you can ask for anything in the world and God will give it to you? Not so fast. Remember that your relationship with God *is* a relationship. Praying for things must be couched in knowing Him, desiring His will and obeying Him. That changes prayer from "Give me this" to "Whatever Your will is."

What about the times He seems to be ignoring your prayers? Well, sometimes God knows that what you want isn't what's best for you. That's hard, isn't it? Remember that He loves you and that His goal is for your heart to grow stronger in trust and love for Him. Don't give up – keep asking, but also keep trusting.

Living it

This is the confidence we have in approaching God: that if we ask anything according to His will, He hears us. And if we know that He hears us – whatever we ask – we know that we have what we asked of Him.

– 1 John 5:14-15

Stay Focused

Jesus replied, "No one who puts a hand to the plow and looks back is fit for service in the kingdom of God."
~ LUKE 9:62

Satan doesn't want you to stay focused. Sometimes life is hard. Jesus knows that you set your heart to serving Him, but then something pulls your attention away – Satan whispers doubts or you begin to question things, or a crisis grabs your attention. Before you know it, your heart has wandered away from trusting God.

It's a daily – no minute-by-minute – choice to stay focused on knowing, loving and serving God. Keep your eyes on Jesus, read His Word, hang on to Him with both hands.

If one hand is pulled away, hang on even tighter until your feet are firmly planted on the Rock of trust once again.

Living it

Dear Father,
It's hard to stay focused on You. I know sometimes it's Satan that sneakily pulls my attention away. But, I confess that sometimes it's just me. I'm not thinking of You at all. I'm sorry, Lord. Please forgive me and help me to be stronger.
In Jesus' name, Amen.

Listen Closely

Jesus called out to them, "Come, follow Me, and I will show you how to fish for people!"

~ MARK 1:17 NLT

Jesus was a master communicator when He lived on this earth. He taught so that His listeners could identify with what He was saying. When Jesus gave this command He was speaking to a group of men who had been fishermen for most of their lives. They understood that He was calling them to the job of bringing others to faith in Jesus.

As you read God's Word and as His Spirit speaks into your heart, it will also be in ways that make sense to you. Listen for His voice calling to you from the midst of your own passions and talents. That's where He will use you in His service.

Living it

What gifts and talents has God given you? What do you enjoy doing? Where are your passions? More than likely, those are the areas He wants you to use in service to Him. Do you see how that can happen?

Comfort vs. Commitment

Jesus answered, "It is written: 'Man shall not live on bread alone, but on every word that comes from the mouth of God.'"

~ MATTHEW 4:4

This was no Spirit-led weight loss plan, but it was forty days with no food. Jesus had been fasting for forty days. He had to be hungry. Satan tempted Him by suggesting He turn stones into bread. Comfort versus commitment. That's one of Satan's best temptations.

Does it ever get to you? You've made a commitment to know and serve God. But when situations make you uncomfortable or you're hungry or frightened, where does that commitment go? Don't get pulled away from Jesus. Stay close to Him. Know His word. Trust His heart. Believe He will take care of your needs – not your wants, but your needs.

Living it

Temptation usually comes in through a door that has been deliberately left open.

– Anonymous

New Life

"You should not be surprised at My saying, 'You must be born again.'"

~ JOHN 3:7

Our human hearts are disconnected from God as a result of sin. We can't do anything about that disconnect except be born again. Jesus says we must have a spiritual rebirth in order to be born into God's kingdom.

The words of this verse are only a few short statements before the famous statement of John 3:16, which pretty much encapsulates the salvation message of Scripture. Believe in Jesus, ask Him to be your Savior, repent of your sins and you will be born again to a new life in God.

Living it

The Christian does not think God will love us because we are good, but that God will make us good because He loves us.

– C. S. Lewis

Urgency

"Open your eyes and look at the fields! They are ripe for harvest."

~ JOHN 4:35

Does it make you a nervous to think about sharing your faith? Are you afraid of rejection? Yes, that could happen. But there are also people who are ready to hear about Jesus' love. They're just waiting for someone to tell them. That's why Jesus said the fields are ripe for harvest. God's desire is that all people would come to know Him.

Look around at the people in your life who don't know Jesus. It's urgent that they hear and have a chance to choose Jesus. Don't be afraid of rejection; be excited at the possibility of opening the door for someone to come into the kingdom.

Living it

Sincerity is the biggest part of selling anything – including the Christian plan of salvation.

– Billy Graham

April

A Good Hunger

"Blessed are those who hunger and thirst for righteousness, for they will be filled."
~ Matthew 5:6

What would our world be like if it were filled with righteousness? There would be no crime. No unfairness. No dishonesty. All people would be treated with honor and respect. A righteous world would be sin free. Well, that isn't going to happen, but that doesn't mean we can't work towards it.

Jesus' words are a challenge to hunger and thirst for God – for the virtuous way of living that righteousness would bring. Pray that it can begin with you. Pray for God to fill you with a hunger and thirst to live righteously.

Living it

The LORD is my shepherd, I lack nothing. He makes me lie down in green pastures, He leads me beside quiet waters, He refreshes my soul. He guides along the right paths for His name's sake.
– Psalm 23:1-3

Us Against Them

"You have heard that it was said, 'Love your neighbor and hate your enemy.' But I tell you, love your enemies and pray for those who persecute you, that you may be children of your Father in heaven. He causes His sun to rise on the evil and the good, and sends rain on the righteous and the unrighteous."

~ MATTHEW 5:43-45

Sometimes people are divided by different beliefs or goals. It makes sense that you are closer to people who agree with you and unfortunately it's a slippery slope to being snarky toward anyone who is different – especially with the current convenience of social media.

Jesus' response to unkind behavior was, "Stop it." Love your enemies as much as you love your friends. God does and He blesses all people, not just the ones who agree with you.

Living it

Dear Father,

Please forgive me, God. I'm so sorry for the way I've treated some people ... even for the thoughts I've had about them. There was no love in those thoughts. I ask for Your help to turn my thoughts around and for those kinder thoughts to be turned into actions.

In Jesus' name, Amen.

Grow Up!

"Be perfect, therefore, as your heavenly Father is perfect."
~ MATTHEW 5:48

Perfect? Was Jesus kidding? No one is perfect except Him, right? The context of this verse seems to be that God's followers should strive to be as perfect as God in loving others. God doesn't lower His standards just to satisfy the cry of, "If you knew her you'd have trouble loving her, too!"

Some people are hard to love. Do you have to love them in order to be perfect? No, but you can ask Him to help you love them. That takes some of the pressure off, doesn't it? His strength is available in helping you become a mature follower of God. Jesus is saying, "Put what I've taught you into practice in your life. Grow more mature in your life with Me."

Living it

Our love to God is measured by our everyday fellowship with others and the love it displays.
– Andrew Murray

All about God

"It was not because of his sins or his parents' sins," Jesus answered. "This happened so the power of God could be seen in him."

~ JOHN 9:3 NLT

People have often questioned why bad things happen to good people. Some think the bad things that happen are punishment for sin. That's what the men talking to Jesus suggested about a man who was born blind. They thought that his blindness was punishment for his parents' sin.

But Jesus turned their thoughts in another direction. What's important is that God is glorified in whatever happens – either by taking away the hardship or by the person's trust in Him during the difficult time. It's all about God, not people.

Living it

Dear Father,
This is a good reminder for me – to give You glory no matter what is going on in my life. It's hard in painful times to remember to give You glory; to realize I can learn and grow a stronger faith through trials. But I know that's true. Thanks for trusting me enough to teach me.

In Jesus' name, Amen.

All the Way In!

Then He said to them all: "Whoever wants to be My disciple must deny themselves and take up their cross daily and follow Me."

~ LUKE 9:23

Jesus didn't promise that the Christian life would be easy. This is His no-holds-barred definition of what it means to follow Him. You've got to be all the way in or you're not in at all.

Being a follower of Jesus means life is all about Him – loving Him, obeying Him, living for Him, learning more about Him. Sure, sometimes life will be difficult because of choices made to follow Him and the consequences that come from others because of those choices. That's OK. The benefits and joy of being Jesus' disciple outweighs all other circumstances.

Living it

Cast your cares on the LORD and He will sustain you; He will never let the righteous be shaken.

– Psalm 55:22

True Rest

"Take My yoke upon you and learn from Me, for I am gentle and humble in heart, and you will find rest for your souls."

~ MATTHEW 11:29

Rest … how wonderful does that sound? When Jesus spoke these words He was addressing the Jews who were being buried under rules and regulations by the Pharisees. Life was heavy and success was not attainable.

Do you ever feel that way? Do you struggle with your marriage, parenting, job responsibilities, following God? Whatever it is that gets you down, just stop. Listen to Jesus' words. Trust Him and ask for His help, strength and guidance. Rest is in that trust and guidance.

Living it

In place of our exhaustion and spiritual fatigue, God will give us rest. All He asks is that we come to Him … that we spend a while thinking about Him, meditating on Him, talking to Him, listening in silence, occupying ourselves with Him – totally and thoroughly lost in the hiding place of His presence.

– Chuck Swindoll

Forgiven Much

"Therefore, I tell you, her many sins have been forgiven – as her great love has shown. But whoever has been forgiven little loves little."

~ LUKE 7:47

This is a warning against self-righteousness. Don't think so much of yourself that you elevate yourself over someone who you perceive to be less righteous (and worthy) than you.

Jesus pointed out a woman who had lived a sinful life – everyone knew she was sinful and yet He forgave her. She realized that she had been forgiven for very much, and she was so very grateful that she worshiped Jesus fully.

Have you honestly faced your own sinfulness? Do you understand how much you have been forgiven? When you do, your love for Jesus will be stronger and your worship will be filled with gratitude.

Living it

Dear Father,

Open my eyes to my own sinfulness. I don't know if I've ever fully realized it. Help me understand it so that I can more deeply appreciate the salvation You have provided. I know that will make me even more passionate about serving You. In Jesus' name, Amen.

Standard of Correctness

"If the blind lead the blind, both will fall into a pit."

~ Matthew 15:14

If you take on the position of leader, make sure you know where you're leading people. The Pharisees thought they knew everything. They fooled themselves into thinking they knew more than God. They lived by rules they made up themselves, instead of obeying God's commands. They insisted that everyone follow their rules or be banned from worshiping. They were truly the blind leading the blind.

Be careful who you follow – test the teachings you receive by their obedience to God's Word. His Word is the final, correct standard of obedience. If you lead, stay true to Scripture and lead by its standard.

Living it

A leader is one who influences a specific group of people to move in a God-given direction.

– J. Robert Clinton

Guard Your Heart

"The things that come out of a person's mouth come from the heart, and these defile them."
~ MATTHEW 15:18

You may know *all* the Christian things to say and even be pretty good about guarding your speech so that those godly things come out most often. But at some point what's really going on in your heart will come out in what you say.

Your words have the power to wound and damage others. Jesus said that the words that fly out of your mouth show what kind of stuff is going on in your heart. If you're selfish, mean-spirited and prideful then all that stuff will show by the words you speak to others. Clean up your heart and your words will clean up, too.

Living it

Dear Father,

I'm embarrassed by some of the words that slide so easily from my lips. I'd like to think You don't hear them; but I know that isn't true. Forgive me, Father. Reveal the places in my heart that need to be cleaned – the places these words grew from.

In Jesus' name, Amen.

Personal Choices

"But what about you?" He asked, "Who do you say I am?"

~ MATTHEW 16:15

Don't you just love Peter? He sometimes spoke before he thought and once in a while that got him into trouble. But there was no doubt that Peter loved Jesus. One time Jesus asked Peter if people were saying that He truly was God's Son. After Peter answered, Jesus asked, "What about you, Peter? Who do you say I am?"

Faith in Jesus is a personal decision. You aren't a Christian just because you go to church once in a while or hang around Christians or even because you read the Bible. You must choose Jesus and you can't ride the fence about it. Who do you say Jesus is?

Living it

How you live your life every day shows your true opinion of who God is.

– Anonymous

Jesus Freak!

"If the world hates you, keep in mind that it hated Me first."
~ JOHN 15:18

The people who hated Jesus the most were the religious leaders. He taught different things than they did and He didn't keep the rules they had themselves made up. Since they hated Jesus, it only made sense that they hated His followers, too. That still happens today.

People who are against God will be against His followers. Sometimes that's good, because you know they recognize you as being obedient to God. Your life might nudge their conscience to also follow Him. Keep on doing what God wants you to do. He will take care of them.

Living it

Have you experienced any level of persecution for your faith? Have you taken a stand for God among your friends? Are you willing to be criticized or made fun of in order to stand strong for Him?

No Room for Pride

"All those who exalt themselves will be humbled, and those who humble themselves will be exalted."

~ LUKE 18:14

There's no room for pride in the heart of a believer. Why? Because everything you have – from intellect to talent to looks – it all comes from God. You had nothing to do with it. Jesus had nothing good to say about people who toot their own horns – braggarts.

Some people think so highly of themselves that they feel they are above other people. They feel entitled to be treated better and to get what they want and to be first all the time. There is nothing in that behavior that shows God's love. Get rid of pride, live humbly as Jesus did.

Living it

It was pride that changed angels into devils; it is humility that makes men as angels.

– St. Augustine

God's whole employment is to lift up the humble and cast down the proud.

– Anonymous

What Are You Hiding?

"Everyone who does evil hates the light, and will not come into the light for fear that their deeds will be exposed."
~ JOHN 3:20

If you do things that you hope no one finds out about, you will definitely want to stick to dark rooms, dark streets, dark corners – places where your behavior will be secret and hidden.

That means you will be trying to hide things from Jesus. He is the true Light, so being close to Him will expose those things you've been trying to hide. What are you hiding? Confess it, let it go … come into the light.

Living it

I am writing you a new command; its truth is seen in Him and in you, because the darkness is passing and the true light is already shining.
– 1 John 2:8

The Pathway of Life

"I am the vine; you are the branches. If you remain in Me and I in you, you will bear much fruit; apart from Me you can do nothing."

~ JOHN 15:5

You can struggle through life trying to accomplish things on your own strength but you'll only frustrate yourself. Do you want to make a difference in this world? Don't try to do it alone. Jesus is the vine. Through Him comes the nutrition to grow your spirit. He gives life, encouragement, hope, forgiveness, wisdom and purpose. Without Him, you can do nothing for God.

Stay connected to Jesus through prayer, Bible reading and quiet thoughtfulness when He can speak into your spirit. Those times give life.

Living it

Dear Father,
I had never thought about my relationship with Jesus as my spiritual food. That makes me see the necessity of staying closely connected so I can grow more mature in my faith. Thank You for this lifeline.

In Jesus' name, Amen.

What Are You Holding on To?

"Go, sell everything you have and give to the poor, and you will have treasure in heaven. Then come, follow Me."
~ MARK 10:21

A rich man came to Jesus and asked how he could have eternal life. Jesus' answer was consistent with what He always taught – love and care for others. In this case He told the rich man to sell everything he owned, then to give the money to the poor. But the wealthy man couldn't let go of his riches. His wealth mattered too much.

The foundation of life with Jesus is loving others. Is there something you're holding onto so tightly that it has become more important than loving others?

Living it

Do all the good you can, by all the means you can, in all the ways you can, in all the places you can, at all the times you can, to all the people you can, as long as ever you can.
– John Wesley

Prove It?

"The Scriptures also say, 'You must not test the LORD your God.'"

~ MATTHEW 4:7 NLT

Satan was tempting Jesus. He was trying to get Jesus to turn away from God and worship him. Satan offered some pretty cool things in tempting Jesus … but none of them worked. Jesus met every temptation with Scripture.

So one of Satan's temptations was to challenge Scripture – to make Jesus prove that God would do what He says He will do. Jesus' response was this verse – don't try to test God. He didn't have to prove anything to Jesus and He doesn't have to prove anything to you. God says He loves you and will take care of you. Believe Him, don't test Him.

Living it

I am convinced that neither death nor life, neither angels nor demons, neither the present nor the future, nor any powers, neither height nor depth, nor anything else in all creation, will be able to separate us from the love of God that is in Christ Jesus our Lord.

– Romans 8:38-39

Lighting the Way

"You are the light of the world. A town built on a hill cannot be hidden."

~ MATTHEW 5:14

We live in a world that strives to be "politically correct." Because of that, some Christians let their standards and even their beliefs be compromised so they can feel more comfortable with the world. Of course, you don't want to be antagonistic or mean in how you treat others, but your light should never be hidden.

Christians – Christ followers – are lights in a dark world: lights that reveal the need for a personal relationship with Christ. Lights of hope. Lights of love. You make a difference by letting your light shine.

Living it

Dear Father,

I want to be a light that makes a difference – a light that reveals Your love to others. It's hard sometimes, like when I'm having a bad day or when I'm tired. Help me to remember that Your love in me makes me a light. May I never take that responsibility lightly.

In Jesus' name, Amen.

Watch Your Words

"I tell you, do not swear an oath at all: either by heaven, for it is God's throne; or by the earth, for it is His footstool; or by Jerusalem, for it is the city of the Great King. And do not swear by your head, for you cannot make even one hair white or black. All you need to say is simply 'Yes' or 'No'; anything beyond this comes from the evil one."

~ MATTHEW 5:34-37

Watch your words. The words that come out of your mouth say a lot about what thoughts are racing through your mind. Do you realize that they also reveal your opinion of who Jesus is?

These words of Jesus are right in the middle of his famous Sermon on the Mount, which gives many instructions on how to live in a way that honors God. Don't be careless with your words. Don't make promises you can't keep. The bottom line is: watch your language. It says a lot about you.

Living it

Dear Father,
It makes me so sad to think that the words I speak may show that I don't really honor You. O Father, I ask You to help me guard my words – to speak kindly and respectfully to others; to speak only words of honor regarding You; to not speak empty, foolish words. Help me, Father, to be cautious.

In Jesus' name, Amen.

Private Prayer

"When you pray, go into your room, close the door and pray to your Father, who is unseen. Then your Father, who sees what is done in secret, will reward you."

~ Matthew 6:6

*A*re you ever self-conscious about praying aloud? Do you think your prayers are too simple compared to other people's elegant words?

Prayer is not a time to be showy because it is a very personal conversation. Prayer is much like when you have a private talk with your best friend and you don't want anyone else to know what you're talking about.

Personal prayer is between you and God. So, keep it private. Jesus says not to make a big show of praying in public about your personal and private requests. Keep it between you and God. He promises to hear and answer.

Living it

The LORD is near to all who call on Him, to all who call on Him in truth.

– Psalm 145:18

Baby Steps

"If you are faithful in little things, you will be faithful in large ones. But if you are dishonest in little things, you won't be honest with greater responsibilities."

~ LUKE 16:10 NLT

$\mathcal{A}$re you the kind of woman who likes a challenge? Do you find yourself looking for the "what's next" in life? Perhaps you have a sincere desire to grow in your usefulness to God's work on this earth and you long for more important or responsible positions.

Jesus made it clear that there are no shortcuts. Prove to God that He can trust you with small jobs and then He will trust you with bigger ones. Be honest with yourself and with God. Learn and grow in faithfulness.

Living it

Not everyone possesses boundless energy or a conspicuous talent. We are not equally blessed with great intellect or physical beauty or emotional strength. But we have all been given the same ability to be faithful.

– Gigi Graham Tchividjian

What Do You Want?

"Unless you people see signs and wonders," Jesus told him, "you will never believe."
~ JOHN 4:48

What do you want from Jesus? Must you see miraculous answers to your prayers or incredible blessings in your life before you will believe in His love and care for you? Can you love Him through the difficult times or the seasons when He seems to be silent? Can you love Him for what His Word says about His care for you?

He loves you. He will take care of you. He will provide your needs. Can you trust Him enough to love Him through the silent times ... through the hard times, when there are no miracles?

Living it

Commit your way to the LORD; trust in Him and He will do this: He will make your righteousness reward shine like the dawn, your vindication like the noonday sun.
– Psalm 37:5-6

Follow Me

After this, Jesus went out and saw a tax collector by the name of Levi sitting at his tax booth. "Follow Me," Jesus said to him.

~ LUKE 5:27

*F*ollow the leader is a fun childhood game. It's fun when it's a game, but as you grow up you start following someone you want to emulate. Some women do follow somebody – even if it's unconsciously.

But problems develop when you choose to follow someone who leads you away from God. Jesus knew that people are followers so He gave simple instructions … follow Him. That leads to peace and happiness.

Living it

I am a committed to-the-death devoted follower of Jesus Christ. I am not a mere "fan" who will walk away when I don't like what He asks me to do or when my "self" disagrees with His solution to a problem in my life.

– Katherine Walden

Loving Others

"I ask you, which is lawful on the Sabbath: to do good or to do evil, to save life or to destroy it?"
~ LUKE 6:9

The religious leaders constantly gave Jesus a hard time. They challenged things He did and things He taught. He even had to defend doing good when it broke rules they were rigid about. The religious leaders were big rule-makers.

What got lost in their world full of rules was love and concern for others – exactly the thing that was tops in Jesus' world! He cared about people much more than man-made rules. The religious leaders could not allow themselves to be flexible enough to put people above rules. How are you doing with that?

Living it

Dear Father,
I ask You to help me care about people as much as You do. Help me to see needs and concerns without people needing to tell me. Father, help me to set aside prejudices and to break through the things that cloud my judgment. Love through me.
In Jesus' name, Amen.

Hear, Believe and Live

"Very truly I tell you, whoever hears My word and believes Him who sent Me has eternal life and will not be judged but has crossed over from death to life."

~ JOHN 5:24

In our politically correct world, some shout that a loving God wouldn't really send anyone to hell. They say there is more than one way to connect with Him – even though Scripture disagrees.

Jesus clearly stated that there is only one pathway to eternal life. It's not tough. It doesn't require a lot of difficult antics to achieve. It's simple … hear God's Word and believe in Jesus. That's it – only one way … Jesus. Have you heard? Have you believed?

Living it

To have faith is to rely upon Christ, the Person, with the whole heart. It is not the understanding of the mind, not theological opinion, not creed, not organization, not ritual. It is the koinonia of the whole personality with God and Christ. This experience of communion with Christ is itself the continual attitude of dependence on the Savior which we call faith.

– Kokichi Kurosaki

God's Forgiveness

"'For this son of mine was dead and is alive again; he was lost and is found.' So they began to celebrate."
~ LUKE 15:24

*D*o you know how very much God loves you? Do you know that even the angels in heaven celebrated when you gave your heart to Him? Do you know that He waited for you to come to Him? Imagine Him waiting at the door for you, as you might wait for your child to come home. He loves you that much.

Perhaps you know the story of the Prodigal Son. Jesus told this story of a father's immediate forgiveness and complete love for his wayward son. It's a beautiful example of God's love and forgiveness of you. He forgives whatever you have done – no questions asked.

What a blessing.

Living it

When was the first time you sensed God's amazing love for you? Can you recall the precious amazement you felt? When is the most recent time you sensed His love? Are you still amazed by His love?

No Judging!

"Do not judge, or you too will be judged."

~ Matthew 7:1

How do you feel when someone makes a judgment about you – fairly or unfairly? Probably not good. Maybe even angry. Maybe you're even tempted to judge her right back.

Having an opinion is one thing, judging is another. Jesus says not to judge. You probably don't have all the information. You don't know the situation, motivation … actually it's just not your place to judge. It's your place to love. After all, that's what Jesus taught. It's hard to judge someone and love them at the same time. If you do, Jesus says you will be judged yourself … by God.

Living it

Dear Father,

I need to confess that judgment bursts out of my heart so quickly. I'm so critical of others and I'm so certain I'm right. Forgive me and clean my heart of its critical spirit. Help me to remember that I don't know what mountains other people are facing and that I need to give them some room.

In Jesus' name, Amen.

Honest Kindnesses

"Be careful not to practice your righteousness in front of others to be seen by them. If you do, you will have no reward from your Father in heaven."

~ MATTHEW 6:1

"Hey, look at me! I'm doing nice stuff for people!" You may know women who seem to broadcast their good deeds. You get the feeling that they wouldn't do them if no one was watching. This is the wrong motivation. Jesus warned against doing good things only for show. Don't do good things just so other people will see you and think you are a wonderful person.

You know that it doesn't matter what other people think. It only matters what Jesus thinks and any "hey-look-at-me" acts don't fool Him. He looks at your heart to see whether or not you are truly compassionate and kind to others. Don't be showy … be honest.

Living it

He gives us more grace. That is why Scripture says: "God opposes the proud but shows favor to the humble."

– James 4:6

Spiritual Lack of Focus

"Let us go somewhere else – to the nearby villages – so I can preach there also. That is why I have come."

~ MARK 1:38

Keeping your focus is not always easy. There's so much work to be done and women are champions at multitasking. You may take on more jobs than you can keep straight. You flit from one to the other and either wear yourself out or don't do your best work.

Jesus knew why He was on earth. He left heaven because He and God had a plan to make a way for people to have a personal relationship with God. Jesus didn't get distracted from what He came to do. He was focused. Focus your time and talents on what God wants you to do … not what other people say you should do.

Living it

How many different tasks, people or responsibilities fill your calendar? Are you doing things you don't really want to do? Are you doing things you know you aren't good at? Maybe it's time to re-evaluate and focus on using the gifts God gave you. If you let some things go, then others who are gifted for those specific tasks can step up and fill the gap.

Step One

"The work of God is this: to believe in the One He has sent."
~ JOHN 6:29

So … you seriously want to be a part of God's work. How do you make that happen? Jesus had one simple answer – believe in Him. Why does He say that? How can you work for someone you don't know?

It's imperative to believe in the truth of the One you are serving and promoting to others. Of course, this sounds pretty basic, but the fact is, if you really believe that Jesus is God's Son then you will change. You will long to know Him, obey Him, and love Him, no matter what life brings. Love and obedience come from a heart that believes in the Savior.

Living it

Consider Jesus. Know Jesus. Learn what kind of person it is you say you trust and love and worship.
– John Piper

It's Urgent

"Repent, for the kingdom of heaven has come near."

~ MATTHEW 4:17

*P*ay attention, people! The kingdom of heaven is all around you. Jesus is with you every minute. Don't just relegate Him to Sunday morning in the sanctuary. Don't block Him out of your daily life. He is a part of every day of your life.

Does this give you a sense of urgency about sharing the message of God's love with those who don't know yet? Good, because Jesus' call to repent – to turn away from sin – to *stop* sinning is a message everyone needs to hear. He is coming again to bring His followers to heaven. Be ready. Tell others so they can be ready, too.

Living it

Do what you can, being what you are. Shine as a glow-worm if you cannot be a star. Work like a pulley if you cannot be a crane; be a wheel grinder if you cannot drive a train. Be the pliant oar if you cannot be the sailor; be the needle if you cannot be a tailor ... Be the sharpened sickle if you cannot be the reaper.

– Anonymous

May

Celebrate!

"How can the guests of the bridegroom fast while he is with them? They cannot, so long as they have him with them."
~ MARK 2:19

Celebrate Jesus. That's what this verse is all about. Celebrate His love. Celebrate His sacrifice. Celebrate His promises. Celebrate His plans for you. Celebrate the promise of eternity. Celebrate always.

Do you find yourself celebrating – or getting bogged down by over-commitments or the pressures of life? He wants you to enjoy Him and the life He gives you. Of course it isn't perfect, but His love and presence in your life is, so … *celebrate*!

Living it

Some Christians have a doom and gloom approach to life. They only see the sin in the world. Jesus encouraged His followers to pay attention to His love for them and for everyone and to celebrate all the wonderful things He has given. Stop right now and think of some of those things. Celebrate Him!

Get Out of Your Box

"It is not the healthy who need a doctor, but the sick."

~ LUKE 5:31

So, you're a pretty good person and you spend most of your time with other pretty good people, right? You stay away from people who are undesirable ... bad influences and all that.

But guess what ... Jesus came for them, too. Yes, they have problems, but that means they need more than ever to hear about God's love, forgiveness and cleansing. Jesus said it – those who are sick need a doctor. He was speaking to the religious leaders who criticized Him for spending time with sinners.

Don't be like those self-righteous critics. Pray for those who need Jesus and when you can ... go to them.

Living it

Dear Father,
I must admit that I don't even know many people who aren't Christians. I stay away from people I feel are really in trouble. I know they need You, but I guess I think it is the job of "professional" Christians to witness to them. I'm sorry for my attitude. Show me how to serve You ... and toward whom I should be serving.

In Jesus' name, Amen.

One Step at a Time

"I have come into the world as a light, so that no one who believes in Me should stay in darkness."
~ JOHN 12:46

*D*o you sometimes wonder which way to turn? The path before you is unclear and you cry out to God for guidance. It's so hard to wait for direction, isn't it? But, if you wait, it will come. It may be only one step in the darkness at a time, but God will illuminate your path.

Jesus is light and He promises that He will not leave you in darkness. Ask Him for guidance and wait for it to come.

Living it

God has wisely kept us in the dark concerning future events and reserved for Himself the knowledge of them, that He may train us up in a dependence upon Himself and a continued readiness for every event.
– Matthew Henry

Worry-Free Zone

"I tell you, do not worry about your life, what you will eat or drink; or about your body, what you will wear. Is not life more than food, and the body more than clothes?"

~ MATTHEW 6:25

Worry is a big speed bump in life. It can easily wiggle into your thoughts. You can try to fight it, but Satan knows where your weakness is. He likes to plant seeds of worry about your family, your lifestyle, your job, your health … whatever it might be.

In tough economic times some worry is for basic things – food, shelter and clothing. That worry pulls you away from trusting God. Jesus says that you don't need to worry about any of it, though. While those things do matter to us, there is a bigger thing to be concerned about – knowing Him; serving Him; loving Him.

Living it

What worry keeps you awake in the middle of the night? Most worries are over things that never happen. Most are things over which you have no control. How can you gain control over worries? Admit them. Give them to Jesus. Let them go.

Be Careful about Judging

"In the same way you judge others, you will be judged, and with the measure you use, it will be measured to you."
~ MATTHEW 7:2

$\mathcal{A}$ judgmental, critical spirit is such a burden. When you think about it, does anyone want to be around someone who is judgmental and critical? Not so much. And, if you're the one living with this kind of spirit, it's oppressive and heavy because you're always finding fault with others instead of loving them as Jesus commanded.

Remember, the measuring stick you use on other people will come back to you, because God is your judge. Don't judge ... just love and let God do the judging.

Living it

Forgiveness is our command. Judgment is not.
– Neil Strait

Just Ask

"What do you want Me to do for you?" He asked.

~ MARK 10:36

How awesome is this? The Son of God asks, "What do you want Me to do for you?" Picture Him sitting in front of you, leaning forward, eyes focused on you, just waiting to hear what you want Him to do for you.

He wants to know because He loves you. He cares about what's troubling you. He cares about your hopes and dreams. He cares. Talk with Him.

Living it

Cast all your anxiety on Him because He cares for you.

– 1 Peter 5:7

Peace Out

"Peace be with you."
~ LUKE 24:36

Sometimes it feels as though the world is crashing down around you. Things on which you had planned don't happen. A job is lost, a loved one dies, a relationship ends, a child rebels … whatever the situation, it pulls you down.

That's probably how Jesus' followers felt when He came to them and said, "Peace be with you." He had just been murdered and everything they thought was going to happen now seemed hopeless. But even in their despair, Jesus came to them. In your moments of despair, He comes to you, too, offering peace. Peace be with you.

Living it

You will keep in perfect peace those whose minds are steadfast, because they trust in You.
– Isaiah 26:3

Dynamic Power

"You will receive power when the Holy Spirit comes on you; and you will be My witnesses in Jerusalem, and in all Judea and Samaria, and to the ends of the earth."

~ ACTS 1:8

*W*hen Jesus returned to heaven He left work for His followers to do. We are to help His kingdom grow by being witnesses of His saving power. It's a big job and kind of scary for some people. But the training program is awesome!

Jesus promised personal, dynamic power for each of us to do this work in the person of the Holy Spirit. The Spirit's presence is hard to understand or explain, but it's real. Jesus promised it. And, if you've ever experienced the reality of His presence in your life, you know it. Call on the Spirit, ask for His help and strength.

Living it

Dear Father,

We don't talk much about the Holy Spirit these days. So I probably don't understand Him as much as I should. Even so, I'm thankful for His presence in my life. I ask you, Father, for the power of the Holy Spirit to fill me – my actions, my words, my hope, my prayers, so that my usefulness in Your work can grow and grow.

In Jesus' name, Amen.

What Is Mercy?

"Blessed are the merciful, for they will be shown mercy."
~ MATTHEW 5:7

Mercy is a word that's used more often in a Christian context than any other place in life. What does mercy look like in everyday life? Mercy is forgiveness, love and patience shown to others, even when it isn't deserved or acknowledged.

These words were spoken during Jesus' Sermon on the Mount. He encouraged, no, commanded His followers to love others. Be kind. Show mercy. Treat others the way you want to be treated. Pay attention to others.

Living it

When a Christian shows mercy, he experiences liberation.
– Warren Wiersbe

Let Go of Anger

"I tell you that anyone who is angry with a brother or sister will be subject to judgment."

~ Matthew 5:22

*A*nger is a selfish emotion because it comes from caring about yourself and how situations affect you and whether you're being treated fairly. Jesus often taught on how people should treat each other.

Just before this statement, He spoke about murder. Jesus brought His teaching down to the simple statement of "Don't be angry." You will be judged for that.

Try to get along with others. Think about others before yourself. Show love to others – your love and God's love. Let Him take care of the situations that tempt you to become angry.

Living it

Temper is what gets most of us into trouble. Pride is what keeps us there.

– Anonymous

Priority Adjustment

"Do not store up for yourselves treasures on earth, where moths and vermin destroy, and where thieves break in and steal."

~ MATTHEW 6:19

*E*verything in this world screams for you to earn more money; get bigger, newer and better stuff; work, work, work. You want to be able to support your family and even keep up with your friends. You don't want to reach retirement age and not be able to afford retirement.

It's such a temptation to focus on earthly treasures. But Jesus reminds us that these efforts should not be at the cost of your spiritual life and your work for Him. What you accumulate here will not matter in eternity. What you do for Him will.

Living it

Dear Father,

You know that life is demanding and busy. I sometimes feel that I'm going from one responsibility to another; just checking things off my to-do list. Time with You, work for You, gets pushed to later or not at all. Please forgive me and help me to reset my priorities.

In Jesus' name, Amen.

Right Priorities

"Store your treasures in heaven, where moths and rust cannot destroy, and thieves do not break in and steal."

~ MATTHEW 6:20 NLT

Jesus said not to store up treasures on earth. Now, what does He mean about treasures in heaven? These treasures may be harder to measure. But, the treasures of heaven come from serving and obeying Him.

You can sense the times when you are doing exactly what He wants you to do; when you're in that sweet spot of being in the center of His will and obeying Him. That's when you are laying up treasure in heaven. Take time to listen to Him and seek His guidance every day. Serve Him with gladness.

Living it

Have you had the experience of sensing that you are in that sweet spot of serving Jesus? It may only be for a season, but it's when you know you're using the talents He gave you at the time and in the place where He wants you. It's an awesome feeling. Be submissive to His guidance so that you may experience this joy.

Honesty Moment

"Where your treasure is, there your heart will be also."
~ MATTHEW 6:21

You can say all the right words. You can show up at church every time the doors open. You can lead Bible studies and teach Sunday school and volunteer with refugees … all good things. But, if you do all those things while your heart is secretly focusing on something else, your treasure is not serving God.

Your treasure is where your heart is focused. Be honest with yourself. What's your motivation for how you spend your time and energy? You're not fooling God, so come clean. Be honest and ask Him to help you get your priorities straight.

Living it

Choose for yourselves this day whom you will serve … But as for me and my household, we will serve the LORD.
– Joshua 24:15

Forgiveness

"If you forgive other people when they sin against you, your heavenly Father will also forgive you."

~ MATTHEW 6:14

*B*ig sigh. Why does Jesus talk about forgiveness so much? Doesn't He realize how hard it is sometimes? Of course He does. However, it's impossible to truly serve God without your human relationships being affected. So, Jesus pointed out that forgiveness is absolutely necessary.

How can you accept or expect His forgiveness if you can't or won't forgive others? As the old saying goes, "it's where the rubber meets the road." Forgive, because you are being forgiven.

Living it

It takes a lot of emotional and psychological energy to keep a wound open, to keep a grudge alive. The longer I allow a wound to fester, the more bitterness, anger and self-pity poison my blood and eat at my heart.

– Albert Haase

The Big Picture

"Look at the birds of the air; they do not sow or reap or store away in barns, and yet your heavenly Father feeds them. Are you not much more valuable than they?"

~ MATTHEW 6:26

Jesus knew that anxiety over the realities of life would consume us sometimes. It's always been a problem – remember the Israelites' concern about hunger and God sending them food from heaven? It's a natural fear and the reality is that people do go hungry. People do lose jobs and homes and even life.

So why did Jesus make this statement? Because you should be able to trust Him with whatever happens. Remember that the picture is bigger than your years on this earth … it's all of eternity. Don't waste time worrying here when you could be learning to know Him and trust Him completely. It's hard, but it's worth it.

Living it

Dear Father,
I'll admit I have trouble with this. There are people around the world who are starving, who don't have clean water … children who live in war zones. Help me to know that You haven't forgotten these people. Help me to see what I might be able to do to help them.
In Jesus' name, Amen.

Pray and Believe

"Do you believe that I am able to do this?"

~ MATTHEW 9:28

When you pray, do you truly believe that God can and will answer your prayer? Scripture tells us to pray in faith – believing.

Don't just toss your prayers out into the air and hope that one of them sticks. Believe that Jesus hears. Believe that He loves. Believe that He will answer. He rewards faith … OK, maybe not in the time frame you would like … but He does answer. And your faith and trust and dependence on Him grows as you pray and believe.

Living it

The prayer of a righteous person is powerful and effective.

– James 5:16

Faith Muscle

"If you have faith as small as a mustard seed, you can say to this mulberry tree, 'Be uprooted and planted in the sea,' and it will obey you."

~ LUKE 17:6

*E*ven a small amount of faith can do big things for God. Faith is like a muscle that grows stronger as it is exercised. When you believe God for a small thing and He does it, then next time you can believe for a bigger thing.

Objects, as the mulberry tree in this statement, obey faith because everything is under God's power. Believe God and if you must start small, then do so. Have faith and see what He does. Exercise that faith muscle!

Living it

Think of a time when you saw your faith in action. What happened? How did you see God move? Did your faith grow stronger after that? Did that help you believe that you can trust God for even bigger things?

Hard Jobs

"My Father, if it is not possible for this cup to be taken away unless I drink it, may Your will be done."

~ MATTHEW 26:42

Jesus was praying in the Garden of Gethsemane. He knew what was ahead and that it was going to be very ugly. He asked God if there was any other way to accomplish what they had planned – which was to make a way for you and me to have a personal relationship with Him.

He was willing to go through the pain and ugliness … for you. He loves you that much. Sometimes doing what's hard is what is needed. Jesus did it for you. He will help you do hard things for Him. Are you willing? He was.

Living it

Dear Father,

I'm humbled and grateful and amazed at the sacrifice of Jesus. Every time I read this verse I realize anew how much You love me. I pray, God, for the courage to do hard things for You – because Jesus did hard things for me.

In Jesus' name, Amen.

Good Intentions

"Watch and pray so that you will not fall into temptation. The spirit is willing, but the flesh is weak."

~ MATTHEW 26:41

You mean well. You mean to be diligent in reading your Bible; in praying, serving. You try your best. But little things wiggle their way into your day. The temptation is to put off doing the "right" things because the "important" things are calling. Your spirit wants to serve God, but your body (actions) gets sidetracked with "stuff."

There's only one way through this … ask God to help you. Ask for His strength and focus to keep you on track. You can try to do it by yourself, but you won't be successful. You need divine assistance.

Living it

Those who hope in the LORD will renew their strength. They will soar on wings like eagles; they will run and not grow weary, they will walk and not be faint.

– Isaiah 40:31

Striking Back

"I tell you, do not resist an evil person. If someone strikes you on the right cheek, turn to them the other cheek also."

~ MATTHEW 5:39

The temptation when someone hurts you is to strike back ... harder. It's a defensive, personal protection mechanism. Jesus tells us to resist that reflex. If someone hurts you, turn the other cheek and give her the chance to do it again.

Why did He say that? Because striking back will truly damage the relationship and He is all about relationships. Forgive and give the other person a chance to make things right. And, if she doesn't, let Jesus take care of her. You keep treating her the way you'd like her to treat you. Is it easy? Not always. Can you do it? Yes, with Jesus' help.

Living it

Dear Father,

You're going to have to help me with this. I tend to want justice right away and feel that I must bring it myself. Help me, Father, to give my relationship issues to You and let You take care of the justice. Thanks.

In Jesus' name, Amen.

Childlike Faith

"Let the little children come to Me, and do not hinder them, for the kingdom of heaven belongs to such as these."
~ MATTHEW 19:14

In Jesus' day, children were not considered very important. So when Jesus said that the kingdom of heaven belongs to people who are like children, that was pretty earthshaking. Why did He say this?

Because children have such simple trust in those they respect. They have faith that trusts Jesus and takes Him at His word. To have faith like a child, don't challenge everything He says ... trust His actions and His promises.

Living it

Dear Father,
I have lots of questions. I have lots of answers as far as what I think You should do. Forgive me, Father, for not being more childlike in my trust. Help me to give up control and just trust You.
In Jesus' name, Amen.

You Are Forgiven

"Your sins are forgiven."

~ LUKE 7:48

Jesus spoke these words to a woman who had anointed Him with expensive perfume, washed His feet with her tears and wiped them dry with her hair. She cared very much for Jesus. Some of the religious leaders criticized her actions, but they showed no respect at all for Him. They had critical, stubborn spirits.

Jesus saw the woman's heart – her devotion to Him and her belief that He was the Messiah. Because of that, He forgave her sin. When Jesus looks into your heart, what does He see? Devotion to Him or a critical, stubborn spirit?

Living it

Dear Father,
I am so thankful for Your forgiveness. I know I don't deserve it. I know You give it every day – even when I don't ask. Thank You for that. Help me, Father, to pass that forgiveness along in my relationships with others.

In Jesus' name, Amen.

Believe Jesus

"Let's go over to the other side of the lake."
~ LUKE 8:22

Jesus and His disciples got into a boat and Jesus said, "Let's go to the other side of the lake." As soon as they sailed, Jesus fell asleep. Then a storm blew up and the disciples became scared that the boat would sink. In terror, they woke Him up. Jesus asked them, "Where's your faith?"

Why did He say that? The trip had begun with Jesus saying, "Let's go over to the other side of the lake." He didn't say, "Let's go half way and then sink." These men didn't trust what He said. Do you believe Jesus' promises? Or do you wake up terrified that He isn't paying attention to your problems?

Living it

Know therefore that the LORD your God is God; He is the faithful God, keeping His covenant of love to a thousand generations of those who love Him and keep His commandments.

– Deuteronomy 7:9

Doing the Right Thing

"Blessed are those who are persecuted because of righteousness, for theirs is the kingdom of heaven."

~ MATTHEW 5:10

In some places around the world Christians are brutally persecuted because of their faith in God. How would you respond to such persecution? Would you stand firm for your faith?

Hopefully you will never have to deal with persecution, but you may find that some people are prickly with you because they know of your Christian walk and it makes them uncomfortable. Will you still stand firm for Jesus? Stand firm; don't compromise Jesus to make other people more comfortable.

Living it!

Comfort and prosperity have never enriched the world as much as adversity has.

– Billy Graham

Take It in Stride

"Blessed are you when people insult you, persecute you and falsely say all kinds of evil against you because of Me."
~ MATTHEW 5:11

Wow, this is a pretty sobering statement. You may be persecuted, insulted and lied about because of your faith in Jesus. That would certainly divide those who are Christians in name only from the Christians who believe in their hearts that Jesus is God's Son and that He died for their sins.

Why would you endure persecution for something you don't really believe in? Standing firm for Jesus will result in blessing. He will be pleased with you. How awesome is that? So, stay close to Him and He will take care of you.

Living it

Christians are severely persecuted and even martyred in some parts of the world. Would you be willing to take a stand for Jesus that might result in persecution or martyrdom? Are you even willing to be criticized or made fun of by people you know? How much does your faith mean to you?

Give Up on Worry

"Do not worry about tomorrow, for tomorrow will worry about itself. Each day has enough trouble of its own."

~ MATTHEW 6:34

*A*re you a worrier? What kinds of things do you worry about? Things that have already happened or things that might possibly happen in the future? You know, of course, that worry of any kind is a waste of energy.

When you worry about things you have no control over, it pulls you away from faith in God because worry and faith can't really hang out in the same space. So, when you feel anxiety and worry creeping into your heart, just stop it. Tell God that you are going to give the situation to Him because you know He can take care of it. Don't waste today worrying about tomorrow.

Living it

Worry is a cycle of inefficient thoughts whirling around a center of fear.

– Corrie ten Boom

Action, Not Words

"Not everyone who says to Me, 'Lord, Lord,' will enter the kingdom of heaven, but only the one who does the will of My Father who is in heaven."

~ MATTHEW 7:21

Some people use God's name all the time but seem to have no clue who He is. They aren't interested in serving Him and they don't love Him. They don't even think about Him much, except maybe when they have a problem. They may be really great at "talking" the Christian faith, but their obedience and service to God is non-existent.

Jesus says those people shouldn't expect to go to heaven. The people who will go to heaven are the ones who obey Him and do what He asks them to do. Are you a talker or a doer?

Living it

What good is it, my brothers and sisters, if someone claims to have faith but has no deeds? Can such faith save them? In the same way, faith by itself, if it is not accompanied by action, is dead.

– James 2:14, 17

A Firm Foundation

"Everyone who hears these words of Mine and puts them into practice is like a wise man who built his house on the rock. The rain came down, the streams rose, and the winds blew and beat against that house; yet it did not fall, because it had its foundation on the rock."

~ MATTHEW 7:24-25

News reports about floods are terrifying. Cars, barns, trees and houses are swept away by the powerful water. Jesus says that houses not built on a firm foundation are most at risk. The rock won't wash away in the water so the house built on it is safer.

Was Jesus talking about construction? What does this mean? He was talking about people – those who hear His teaching, obey it and put it into practice in their lives are wise – just like the man who built his house on rock. Where's your foundation?

Living it

"This is love for God: to keep His commands."

– 1 John 5:3

Inside Out

"Are you so dull?" He asked. "Don't you see that nothing that enters a person from the outside can defile them?"
~ MARK 7:18

What's in your heart comes out in your words and actions. Don't try to blame your sins on situations or people around you. Sin comes from the heart. When you decide in your heart to be mean or to cheat or lie – that's sin. That choice is made, because your heart doesn't feel it's wrong.

So what lives on the inside comes out in your actions. Give your heart to Jesus and ask Him to reveal the good and bad in your heart and to cleanse away your sin.

Living it

Create in me a pure heart, O God, and renew a steadfast spirit within me.
– Psalm 51:10

Relationships

"Love your enemies, do good to them, and lend to them without expecting to get anything back. Then your reward will be great, and you will be children of the Most High, because He is kind to the ungrateful and wicked."

~ LUKE 6:35

Relationships. Jesus focused much of His teaching on relationships. Be kind to your enemies, He said. Love them. Help them in any way you can. Don't worry about getting even with people who hurt you. Be even kinder and more helpful to them than you are to your friends.

Why? Anyone can be nice to her friends. A God-follower will go the extra mile and be kind to her enemies too.

Living it

Revenge ... is like a rolling stone, which, when a man hath forced up a hill, will return upon him with a greater violence, and break those bones whose sinews gave it motion.

– Albert Schweitzer

Above All Love

"God did not send His Son into the world to condemn the world, but to save the world through Him."
~ JOHN 3:17

Following God does not mean a life of rule-following and having your hand slapped every time you do something wrong. Too often that is the perception of those who resist following Christ. Sometimes that perception is because of the condemnation and criticism from Christians.

Christ came to teach. He came to love. He came to challenge people to turn from their sinfulness. He came to save the world from itself and to encourage believers to live a life of love, acceptance and eternity with Him.

Living it

Dear Father,
Thank You for loving me so much. Sometimes Satan tempts me to get stuck in the fact that I "have" to follow rules and then I forget the love and that You just want to know me and let me know You.
In Jesus' name, Amen.

June

Taking Care of Business

"How can you say to your brother, 'Let me take the speck out of your eye,' when all the time there is a plank in your own eye?"

~ MATTHEW 7:4

Facing your own sinfulness is much harder than pointing out someone else's problems. But in a world that is to be blanketed in God's love, Jesus points out the foolishness of criticizing a friend's small transgression when you are ignoring your own much bigger problem.

Sure, it's tempting to try to "fix" someone else, but the reality is that her issues are between her and God. Take care of your own problems before telling someone else how to fix theirs.

Living it

The course of thy life will speak more for thee than the discourse of thy lips.

– George Swinnock

No Shortcuts

"If you are offering your gift at the altar and there remember that your brother or sister has something against you, leave your gift there in front of the altar. First go and be reconciled to them; then come and offer your gift."

~ MATTHEW 5:23-24

Jesus is again focusing on relationships. He tells us not to try and take a shortcut to intimacy with God by ignoring relationships with people. Offering your gifts to God when you have problems with others will just not work. God cares about how you and your friends and family get along.

So, if someone is angry with you – whether you did anything wrong or not – work it out. Go and talk to her and apologize if you need to. Once those relationships are good, then give your gifts to God. Don't expect Him to bless you if you are trying to shortcut relationships with others.

Living it

Make every effort to keep the unity of the Spirit through the bond of peace.

– Ephesians 4:3

Showing Christ's Love

"If you love those who love you, what reward will you get? Are not even the tax collectors doing that? And if you greet only your people, what are you doing more than others? Do not even pagans do that?"

~ MATTHEW 5:46-47

Of course you love those who love you – family and friends. That's a no-brainer. Perhaps you even pride yourself on seeking out visitors to church and greeting them.

Where reality sinks in is in how you treat a store assistant, a waitron at the restaurant, the desk clerk at the DMV. How about the homeless person at the train stop every day? Or the people who picket outside government offices for causes you don't agree with? Going the extra mile to show love to those people – or whatever people you have trouble loving – that's showing Christ's love ... and being obedient to Him.

Living it

Dear Father,

I needed this reminder today to have a loving attitude to all people I meet throughout the course of my day. Help me, Father, to remember that I can spread seeds of kindness and love to everyone.

In Jesus' name, Amen.

Prayer — Lesson One

"This, then is how you should pray: 'Our Father in heaven, hallowed be Your name.'"

~ MATTHEW 6:9

Jesus gave an example of prayer. Notice that in the Lord's Prayer, the first thing He did was honor God's name. So often our prayers begin with requests.

While God does want to hear the things that are on our hearts, it is good to step back and recognize His holiness and the honor due Him. Respect His name above all others. Keep Him in a place of respect and honor as you begin your prayer time.

Living it

Dear Father,
You are holy. You are powerful. You are loving. You are pure. You are awesome. I forget to recognize these things and other amazing things about You sometimes. I'm sorry that I often go right to my requests or complaints. Forgive me, most awesome, forgiving and loving Father.

In Jesus' name, Amen.

A Second Lesson in Prayer

"Your kingdom come, Your will be done, on earth as it is in heaven."

~ MATTHEW 6:10 NLT

Jesus continued His prayer lesson with the example that we should give up control of our own lives by being submissive to God's will.

Actually, He went even farther than submission; He asked that God's will be done on earth. That means asking for God's will in your life … in the lives of people you love … all around you. This shows complete trust in Him and faith in the goodness of His plan for all things.

Living it

The will of God for your life is simply that you submit yourself to Him each day and say, "Father, Your will for today is mine. Your pleasure for today is mine. Your work for today is mine. I trust You to be God. You lead me today and I will follow."

– Kay Arthur

One Day at a Time

"Give us today our daily bread."

~ MATTHEW 6:11

*T*he Lord's Prayer that Jesus taught His followers asks God to supply our daily needs … just what is needed for this day. Ask for the food you need for this day; the help you need for this day; the comfort and strength you need for this day – not tomorrow or next week or a year from now.

Don't worry about the future and don't ask to stockpile God's blessings. Trust God to meet your needs one day at a time.

Living it

Dear Father,
Thank You for meeting my daily needs. Thank You for the many times You not only meet my needs, but also my wants. Your blessings are abundant and constant. Thank You so much.

In Jesus' name, Amen.

Prayer and Relationships

"Forgive us our debts, as we also have forgiven our debtors."
~ MATTHEW 6:12

Jesus began the Lord's Prayer by honoring God's name; then He gave all control to God. Next, He asked God
Now, He asks God for forgiveness. But the prerequisite to that request is forgiving others. So this example shows that we shouldn't ask God to do things for us that we aren't willing to do for others. Remember that Jesus always focused on relationships. It is pointless to come to God with praise or requests if there are relationship issues you aren't willing to deal with.

Living it

Forgiveness is not that stripe which says, "I will forgive, but not forget." It is not to bury the hatchet with the handle sticking out of the ground, so you can grasp it the minute you want it.

– Dwight L. Moody

Prayer and Temptation

"Lead us not into temptation, but deliver us from the evil one."

~ Matthew 6:13

God will never lead you into temptation. You may lead yourself or Satan may lead you. That's why Jesus taught us to pray for protection from temptation. It will come. You can bank on that.

The closer you follow Jesus, the more temptation you will face. Satan sneaks into your mind and heart and tempts you to do things you know are disobedient to God. So Jesus teaches us to pray that God will protect us from those temptations.

Living it

The temptations in your life are no different from what others experience. And God is faithful. He will not allow the temptation to be more than you can stand. When you are tempted, He will show you a way out so that you can endure.

– 1 Corinthians 10:13 NLT

Someday ...

"My Father's house has many rooms; if that were not so, would I have told you that I am going there to prepare a place for you? And if I go and prepare a place for you, I will come back and take you to be with Me that you also may be where I am."

~ JOHN 14:2-3

Praise God – life on this earth is not the end. Jesus promised that when He returned to heaven He would prepare a place for you and then to come and fetch you so that you can be with Him there.

In the meantime, you have the responsibility and opportunity to know Jesus better and better and to grow in obedience and service to Him. That kind of living lays up treasures in heaven.

Being a Christian is not just about heaven … it's about knowing Jesus in a real and personal way.

Living it

He who is the faithful witness to all these things says, "Yes, I am coming soon."

– Revelation 22:20 NLT

The Way to Heaven

"I am the way, the truth, and the life. No one can come to the Father except through Me."

~ JOHN 14:6 NLT

*T*oday more than ever there are people who insist that there are several pathways to knowing God – they say that Jesus is not the only way. They are wrong.

Jesus made it very clear that the only way to know God is to believe that He is God's Son, who died for your sins, and is now in heaven with God. God made the way to heaven so simple – just accept Jesus as Savior, confess your sins to Him and invite Him to live in your heart – that's the way, the truth and the life.

Living it

Have you asked Jesus to be your Savior? Have you confessed your sin to Him and repented – turned away from sin? Of course sin still happens, but He is the way, the truth and the life and He will teach you daily how to turn away from sin. He is life.

The Real Thing

"Anyone who loves Me will obey My teaching. My Father will love them, and We will come to them and make Our home with them."

~ JOHN 14:23

*A*thletes thank God when they have a great victory. People who have survived a crisis mention the "Big Guy" who watched out for them. Many people call on God in a crisis or sing His praises when things go well.

But do these people really, honestly know God and love Him in a personal way? Jesus said there is one true evidence that people love Him – obedience to Him. Just reading His Word, and even knowing His Teachings is not enough. You have to put it into action in your life.

Living it

"Obey Me, and I will be your God, and you will be My people. Do everything as I say, and all will be well!"

– Jeremiah 7:23 NLT

Hear, Receive, Act

"A farmer went out to plant his seed. As he scattered it across his field, some seed fell on a footpath, where it was stepped on, and the birds ate it … This is the meaning of the parable: The seed is God's Word. The seeds that fell on the footpath represent those who hear the message, only to have the devil come and take it away from their hearts and prevent them from believing and being saved."

~ LUKE 8:5, 11-12 NLT

Isn't it wonderful that Jesus told stories to illustrate His lessons? Stories make the lesson so much more understandable.

This story explained what happens when people hear the Word of God, but don't immediately grab it with their hearts. They just look at it without receiving it. That gives the devil a chance to snatch the truth away so that they do not believe in Jesus. He's always waiting to do that. Hear God's Word. Receive it. Put it into action in your life.

Living it

Dear Father,
I pray for Your Word to come alive in my heart. I pray for Your love to take root in me so that my relationship with You can grow stronger and I can become the woman of God You desire for me to be. Help me, Father.

In Jesus' name, Amen.

A Good Root System

"Some fell on rocky ground, and when it came up, the plants withered because they had no moisture ... Those on the rocky ground are the ones who receive the Word with joy when they hear it, but they have no root. They believe for a while, but in the time of testing they fall away."

~ LUKE 8:6, 13

Roots. A plant cannot survive without a good root system to bring nourishment and water. In this story, people who gladly accept Jesus, but don't grow by spending time with Him, reading the Bible and praying, do not develop a good root system.

So when problems come, they have nothing to grab on to. Their relationship with Jesus is all surface. Jesus reminds us to not neglect the importance of being fed so your faith can grow stronger and stronger.

Living it

People can't see your root system, but God can.

– Warren Wiersbe

Strangled Faith

"Other seed fell among thorns that grew up with it and choked out the tender plants ... The seeds that fell among the thorns represent those who hear the message, but all too quickly the message is crowded out by the cares and riches and pleasures of this life. And so they never grow into maturity."

~ LUKE 8:7, 14 NLT

Oh yes, you know what this is like, don't you? The worries of life push in front of trust, hope and faith. They get in the way of growing faith and strangle any chance for new growth by that little niggle in your brain that questions every thought of trust.

Jesus teaches that people who hear the message of God's love but still let worry and other things take over their hearts and minds are like those seeds that fell among thorns. The truth of God's love gets pushed aside by the worries of life so they do not grow strong in their faith.

Living it

People gather bundles of sticks to build bridges they never cross.

– Anonymous

Perseverance

"Still other seed fell on good soil. It came up and yielded a crop, a hundred times more than was sown ... But the seed on good soil stands for those with a noble and good heart, who hear the Word, retain it, and by persevering produce a good crop."

~ LUKE 8:8, 15

*T*he key word in the description of this kind of seed is persevering. Jesus was describing good seed – which is people who receive the message of God's love and begin to grow in faith.

Some people think that once they accept Jesus their lives will be easy and crisis-free. But that isn't true. There will still be problems. However, they persevere – fight through the problems by staying close to Jesus and letting Him help them stay true and trusting His will for their lives.

Living it

Let perseverance finish its work so that you may be mature and complete, not lacking anything.

– James 1:4

Humility

"Blessed are the meek, for they will inherit the earth."

~ MATTHEW 5:5

Meekness is a quality that is definitely not touted as something today's women should strive for. No, women are told to be strong, powerful and assertive. Those are the women who make a "mark" in the world. Except … that's not what Jesus says. He says that a meek (humble) person who puts others' needs ahead of her own will be blessed.

Just as always, Jesus' teaching is focused on love for others and for God. Of course, this doesn't mean a woman can't be self-confident; but not at the cost of disregarding others.

Living it

Dear Father,

Show me how to be meek while also standing firm for You. Show me how to put others' needs ahead of my own so that Your love comes through without becoming an enabler to others' problems. It's a fine line, God. I need Your help to see where it is.

In Jesus' name, Amen.

Living with Purpose

The Spirit of the LORD is on me, because He has anointed me to bring Good News to the poor. He has sent me to proclaim that captives will be released, that the blind will see, that the oppressed will be set free, and that the time of the LORD's favor has come.

~ LUKE 4:18-19 NLT

Jesus knew why He came to earth. He didn't come only to die for our sins. He had an even broader purpose – to teach people how to live and preach God's love and help all to know God and live in obedience to Him … all so you would know how to live in a way that honors and pleases God.

Do you know your purpose? Do you know how God has prepared you to serve Him … what your talents and gifts are? More than likely He desires your service through those gifts. Are you living with purpose and serving Him?

Living it

We ourselves feel that what we are doing is just a drop in the ocean. But the ocean would be less because of that missing drop.

– Mother Teresa

The Kingdom Is Near

"The Kingdom of God is near! Repent of your sins and believe the Good News!"

~ MARK 1:15 NLT

It may be hard to imagine but life on this planet is just a blip in the realm of all eternity so, yes, the kingdom of God is near. Eternity is near. Jesus encouraged those who heard Him and those who read His words to repent and believe.

Be ready to enjoy eternity with Him. But not only that, enjoy the here and now in His presence in your life, guiding, teaching, growing and blessing you to become the woman of God that is His dream for you!

Living it

Let us consider how we may spur one another on toward love and good deeds.

– Hebrews 10:24

Few Words, Great Meaning

"When you pray, do not keep on babbling like pagans, for they think they will be heard because of their many words."
~ MATTHEW 6:7

Prayer is such a mystery. Private, personal prayer is one thing because that's just between you and God. But are you shy about praying in public? Is it anxiety-inducing because you feel inadequate that your prayers seem so simple and you aren't able to put together flowery phrases as some people do? That's OK.

Jesus is just fine with simple, heartfelt prayers that share the concerns, fears, blessings and joys in your life. Just tell Him what you're feeling and thinking. Maybe sometimes you don't even know what to pray, but can only utter a word or a name. That's also fine, your prayers do not need to be fancy – just from your heart.

Living it

There is no wonder more supernatural and divine in the life of a believer than the mystery and ministry of prayer ... the hand of the child touching the arm of the Father and moving the wheel of the universe.

– A. B. Simpson

Respect for God's House

"Get these out of here! Stop turning My Father's house into a market!"

~ JOHN 2:16

Treat God's house with respect. This has become confusing with churches meeting in strip malls or warehouses. Some churches have coffee and pastries readily available and people come to services dressed very casually.

Jesus' words go even deeper because He saw people in the temple who were making a profit by cheating poor people. God's house is for all people – rich, poor, new believer, old saint, young and old. Let all feel welcome there and above all, honor God in your words and actions.

Living it

Dear Father,
Help me to honor Your house and treat it with respect. It doesn't matter if our church meets in a warehouse or a mall or a park – it is the place where I gather with other believers to worship You and that makes it a place worthy of honor and respect.

In Jesus' name, Amen.

Generosity and Unselfishness

"Give to the one who asks you, and do not turn away from the one who wants to borrow from you."

~ MATTHEW 5:42

Jesus taught that it is pointless to spend all your energy trying to get even with people who hurt you. It's not important to always try to come out on top in an argument. It is more important to save the relationship rather than to win a battle.

In fact, go the extra mile and when someone, even someone who isn't a friend, wants to borrow something from you or asks you for something, give it to them. In fact, give them more than they ask for. Show generosity and unselfishness to all.

Living it

For it is in giving that we receive.
– St. Francis of Assisi

Real Rest

"Come with Me by yourselves to a quiet place and get some rest."

~ MARK 6:31

Jesus was constantly surrounded by large crowds of people. Many of them wanted to see Him do miracles more than they wanted to hear what He taught. The large crowds made it hard for Jesus and His disciples to get any down time. In fact, right before this, Jesus' disciples had just told Him that they hadn't even had time to eat.

Jesus cared about them just as He cares about you and He knows that one basic thing that's good to do is to get away from the chaos of life and just be alone with Him for a while. Take time to have quiet time with just you and God. That will give you rest.

Living it

How are you doing at creating space in your life for alone time with Jesus? Do you make time besides the moments when you are driving in your car? Are you thinking, "I don't have time to make time?" How about these options? Can you get up a few minutes early? Can you cut back on social media time? Just those two things can possibly give you several minutes a day.

Promises Fulfilled

"Do not think that I have come to abolish the Law or the Prophets; I have not come to abolish them but to fulfill them."
~ MATTHEW 5:17

The Old Testament was written before Jesus ever came to earth, but several of its writers predicted His coming. Jesus knew the Old Testament teachings and He was the bridge between the Old Testament and the New Testament. Everything the Old Testament predicted was fulfilled by Jesus!

It's important to study both the Old and New Testaments and to thank God for the promises made that were fulfilled.

Living it

"At that time I will gather you; at that time I will bring you home. I will give you honor and praise among all the peoples of the earth when I restore your fortunes before your very eyes," says the LORD.
– Zephaniah 3:20

God's Love for You

"Suppose one of you has a hundred sheep and loses one of them. Doesn't he leave the ninety-nine in the open country and go after the lost sheep until he finds it?"

~ LUKE 15:4

God loves you so very much. You. Not just "the world." But YOU. In case you ever feel that you aren't important to Him, Jesus told this story to give an example of how much God loves each and every person.

You may feel as though you're lost in the crowd sometimes, but every person is important to God and He will search high and low to make sure everyone has a chance to know Him. As Jesus said, God would leave the crowd to go look for one follower who has wandered away.

Living it

Dear Father,
All I can say is thank You. Thank You for Your love. Your love makes me feel so special. I know that You love me enough to search me out and guide me back to You when I'm lost. I'm amazed by Your love.

In Jesus' name, Amen.

Love God First

"You will always have the poor among you, but you will not always have Me."

~ JOHN 12:8

Does this seem like an odd statement for Jesus to make? After all, didn't He often encourage His followers to love and care for others? Yes, He did. But, don't forget that Jesus also taught that there is nothing more important than loving, honoring and serving God.

So, He is saying here not to let anything or anyone become more important than God. You see, the thing is that if you are serious about loving and serving Him, then you will automatically take care of the poor – that kind of love and care grows out of a heart that loves Jesus.

Living it

Let this be thy whole endeavor, this thy prayer, this thy desire, that thou mayest be stripped of all selfishness, and with entire simplicity follow Jesus only.

– Thomas à Kempis

Your Assignment ...

"Go and make disciples of all nations, baptizing them in the name of the Father and of the Son and of the Holy Spirit, and teaching them to obey everything I have commanded you. And surely I am with you always, to the very end of the age."

~ MATTHEW 28:19-20

Jesus' instructions are for His followers to make disciples by sharing the message of God's love and Jesus' sacrifice with everyone.

In the original Greek, this statement says, "As you are going, or in your going ..." So, wherever you go and whatever you do ... be sharing. Be intentional.

Does that mean you should preach? Not necessarily, but you should use the gifts and talents He has given you. Do these instructions seem overwhelming? Don't worry – Jesus says that He will be with you – always.

Living it

Everyone has a responsibility to share the message of God's love and to teach new believers to know Him better so they can obey Him and live for Him. You never have to be afraid that you can't do the work because Jesus is with you ... always.

True Authority!

"The Son of Man has authority on earth to forgive sins."
~ MARK 2:10

It's hard to imagine, but the religious leaders of His day constantly criticized Jesus. They actually looked for ways to trick Him in order to prove that He broke the religious laws of the Old Testament. But, of course, he didn't. They questioned by whose authority He could tell a man that His sins were forgiven.

Jesus never let them get to Him. He answered their accusations with statements like this proclaiming that He has the authority of God to forgive sins. Thank God for that authority.

Living it

Dear Father,
I'm so grateful that I can trust Your authority to forgive my sins. I believe that You wash me clean each time I confess my sins to You. Please help me to be able to forgive myself so that I can start fresh each day for You.
In Jesus' name, Amen.

Mercy, Not Sacrifice

"It is not the healthy who need a doctor, but the sick. But go and learn what this means: 'I desire mercy, not sacrifice.' For I have not come to call the righteous, but sinners."

~ MATTHEW 9:12-13

Jesus desires mercy, not sacrifice. What does that mean? He doesn't want your money. He doesn't even want your time and energy if it isn't wrapped in mercy shown to those around you – kindness to all, not only your friends; forgiveness for those who wrong you; understanding for those who disagree with you.

People who think they have everything figured out and that they are always right do not think they need help. Sinners know they do.

Living it

If Christ does not reign over the mundane events in our lives, He does not reign at all.

– Paul Tripp

Nothing in Return

"If you lend to those from whom you expect repayment, what credit is that to you? Even sinners lend to sinners, expecting to be repaid in full."

~ LUKE 6:34

Once again, Jesus drives home the point that treating others as you would like to be treated is key to serving Him. Look at the people around you and ask, "What can I do for someone else?" … not "what can I gain from them?"

Are you willing to help those who can give you nothing in return? If you treat your friends with generosity … so what? Anyone can do that. But if you unselfishly reach out to those with whom you do not have a relationship and show mercy to them, that is God's love in action. Mercy helps others and expects nothing in return. It is a different kind of love than the world recognizes.

Living it

Anyone who proposes to do good must not expect people to roll stones out of his way, but must accept his lot calmly, even if they roll a few stones upon it.

– Albert Schweitzer

Private Service

"Give your gifts in private, and your Father, who sees everything, will reward you."

~ MATTHEW 6:4 NLT

Why do you do what you do? Teach Sunday school? Work with refugees? Lead a Bible study? Help out at an animal shelter? Whatever you do to serve God, why do you do it? If no one else knew what you were doing – giving or praying – would you still do it?

The Christian life is not about showing off. Helping others, being generous, sacrificing for someone else – those are all good things. But if you live that way just so people will say, "Wow, what a generous person," then that's all the reward you'll get. Do things privately so that only you and God know about your generosity.

Living it

Nothing disciplines the inordinate desires of the flesh like service, and nothing transforms the desires of the flesh like serving in hiddenness. The flesh whines against service but it screams against hidden service. It strains and pulls for honor and recognition.

– Richard Foster

July

The Kingdom of God

"I assure you, no one can enter the Kingdom of God without being born of water and the Spirit."

~ JOHN 3:5 NLT

Nicodemus had questions for Jesus about the things He taught. He was a religious leader, but, like most of the religious leaders, he didn't understand the spiritual side of Jesus' teaching. They lived their lives by laws, not by faith.

Jesus said that a person had to be born of the Spirit and that made no sense to them. Jesus explained that when you believe in Him, the Holy Spirit comes in and lives in a person's heart, leading, guiding and loving. That makes one a part of God's kingdom – so much easier than living by rules.

Living it

"You will receive power when the Holy Spirit comes on you; and you will be My witnesses in Jerusalem, and in all Judea and Samaria, and to the ends of the earth."

– Acts 1:8

Jesus Is the Light

"This is the verdict: Light has come into the world, but men loved darkness instead of light because their deeds were evil."

~ JOHN 3:19

Jesus is the Light of the world. Read that again – Jesus is the LIGHT OF THE WORLD. He is the light that reveals selfishness, hatred, dishonesty, laziness … whatever people may try to hide in the darkness, it is revealed when Jesus is close.

Some people respond to that by asking Jesus to clean up their hearts. Some say, "No way, I like the way I am." Those are the ones Jesus is talking about here. They choose the darkness instead of the light, because they like doing evil things.

Be brave enough to let Jesus reveal any darkness that may be lingering in your heart.

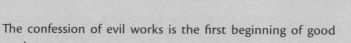

Living it

The confession of evil works is the first beginning of good works.

– St. Augustine

Glory to God

"Whoever lives by the truth comes into the light, so that it may be seen plainly that what he has done has been done through God."

~ JOHN 3:21

Truth is found in obeying God's Word. If a person lives by that truth, then she has nothing to hide. So she is willing to step into the light and know that God sees everything – the good and the bad. She is willing to let everyone around her see who she is and to declare that the changes in her heart and life are all due to Christ and His power and love. This woman wants everyone to know that her good deeds are because of Him. She gives all the glory to God.

Living it

Dear Father,
I have to admit that sometimes I do want to stay in the shadows so I can "hide" my true self from You. But, I know that You know all of me anyway. Help me to really see my actions, to own them, to confess them and to turn away from them.
In Jesus' name, Amen.

Number One

"'Love the Lord your God with all your heart and with all your soul and with all your mind.' This is the first and greatest commandment."

~ MATTHEW 22:37-38

We read in the Old Testament that God is a jealous God. He will not share your heart with anything or anyone else. He desires that you love Him with *all* your heart. Jesus emphasized that when He left no room for compromise.

Love God completely. Give Him your heart – your emotions. Give Him your soul – your being. Give Him your mind – your thoughts. He wants to be Number One in your life … simply because you are Number One in His.

Living it

The LORD Your God is a consuming fire, a jealous God.

– Deuteronomy 4:24

The Second Commandment

"The second [commandment] is like it: 'Love your neighbor as yourself.' All the Law and the Prophets hang on these two commandments."

~ MATTHEW 22:39-40

Jesus said that loving God with all your heart, soul and mind is the greatest commandment. Now He follows that up by saying that the second greatest commandment is to love others. Wait, not just love them, but love them like you love yourself.

What does that mean? Well, what do you do for yourself? Keep yourself safe, provide for yourself – kind of make the self your focus, right? Jesus says to do the same for others. Love is what it's all about.

Living it

Intense love does not measure, it just gives.

– Mother Teresa

Comfort

"Peace I leave with you; My peace I give you. I do not give to you as the world gives. Do not let your hearts be troubled and do not be afraid."

~ JOHN 14:27

When life gets stressful and your problems are overwhelming, what do you long for? Peace, right? You want the fear to go away.

Some people look for peace in their friends, their jobs, financial success, power … but none of that will last. Only Jesus gives real peace and takes away all fear. All you have to do is trust Him and lean on Him. Come to this verse when life bears down on you. Do not let your heart be troubled. Do not be afraid. Find comfort and peace in Jesus.

Living it

Now may the Lord of peace Himself give you peace at all times and in every way. The Lord be with all of you.

– 2 Thessalonians 3:16

Protection

"My prayer is not that You take them out of the world but that You protect them from the evil one."
~ JOHN 17:15

The more you try to live for Jesus, the harder Satan will come after you. If he can pull you away from Jesus through discouragement or disappointment, he will. Jesus knows what Satan is up to because He prays for your protection. He could have just asked God to take all Christians to heaven but He didn't because Christians have work to do here on earth – telling others about God's love.

So when life gets tough and you sense Satan's attacks, remember that Jesus is praying for you and that God will protect you.

Living it

Dear Father,
Just the knowledge that Jesus prays for me gives me so much peace. Jesus loves me. He prays for me and I know that You answer that prayer every day in countless ways. Help me to remember that Jesus prays for me and that You are watching out for me.
In Jesus' name, Amen.

Jesus' Broken Heart

"My soul is overwhelmed with sorrow to the point of death. Stay here and keep watch with Me."

~ MATTHEW 26:38

Jesus took His disciples with Him to the Garden of Gethsemane on the night He was to be arrested. Imagine how He must have felt. He knew what was coming – betrayal, arrest, torture, death.

Why was His soul overwhelmed with such sorrow? Because of the pain that was ahead for Him? Maybe. But He also may have felt sorrow because of the people who heard Him teach and knew of His miracles but had still rejected Him and the message of God's love. His heart was broken out of love for them. He longs for all people to know Him.

Living it

"God loved the world so much that He gave His one and only Son, so that everyone who believes in Him will not perish but have eternal life."

– John 3:16 NLT

Prayer

"Everyone who asks, receives. Everyone who seeks, finds. And to everyone who knocks, the door will be opened."
~ MATTHEW 7:8 NLT

Do you take prayer seriously? Do you believe God hears you? Do you believe He will answer? Prayer is such a privilege; it is an opportunity to talk to Almighty God and tell Him what's on your heart. He wants to know! That's why Jesus made the point of telling you that asking, seeking and knocking brings results.

Will He give you everything you ask for? Probably not, because He sees the bigger picture of your life and experiences. But He knows what is best for you. He will listen and He will be with you through whatever things weigh on your heart.

Living it

No learning can make up for the failure to pray. No earnestness, no diligence, no study, no gifts will supply its lack.
– E. M. Bounds

Secret Christians?

"No one lights a lamp and then puts it under a basket. Instead, a lamp is placed on a stand, where it gives light to everyone in the house."

~ MATTHEW 5:15 NLT

When something amazing happens to you, do you call your family and friends to share the news? Sure, you want everyone to know so they can share your joy. Shouldn't that be how Christians feel about Jesus?

There should be a thrill; amazement and gratitude and joy about His love that the news just spills out. Christians should want to share it with others. It should truly be impossible to be a secret Christian, right?

Living it

We should not ask, "What is wrong with the world?" for that diagnosis has already been given. Rather, we should ask, "What has happened to the salt and light?"

– John R. W. Stott

Honoring God's Word

"Truly I tell you, until heaven and earth disappear, not the smallest letter, not the least stroke of a pen, will by any means disappear from the Law until everything is accomplished."
~ MATTHEW 5:18

Think about what the Bible has dealt with through the centuries – severe persecution and the efforts to completely destroy it. The Bible has persevered because God protected it. It is His Word and He wanted it to be available for people to read so they could know Him and how He has interacted with His creation since the beginning.

The Bible is so very important to God and obviously to Jesus. Is it important to you? How much you value it says a lot about your relationship with God.

Living it

All Scripture is God-breathed and is useful for teaching, rebuking, correcting and training in righteousness, so that the servant of God may be thoroughly equipped for every good work.
– 2 Timothy 3:16-17

Obedience Matters

"Anyone who sets aside one of the least of these commands and teaches others accordingly will be called least in the kingdom of heaven, but whoever practices and teaches these commands will be called great in the kingdom of heaven."

~ MATTHEW 5:19

God doesn't take disobedience lightly. He urges and expects His children to know and obey Scripture. Not only that, He expects His children to teach others to obey and definitely not to lead them away from obeying it.

Obeying makes life better. It brings better relationships with others, and honor to God. It brings self-respect and care for yourself. Those who honor Scripture will be honored in heaven. Those who do not, and encourage others to also disobey, will answer for that in heaven.

Living it

Dear Father,

I'm sorry for the times my words or actions have led people away from You rather than closer to You. Please forgive me and help me, Father, to measure my words and deeds so that they bring honor to You and show You to those around me.

In Jesus' name, Amen.

The High Road

"Settle matters quickly with your adversary who is taking you to court. Do it while you are still together on the way, or your adversary may hand you over to the judge, and the judge may hand you over to the officer, and you may be thrown into prison. Truly I tell you, you will not get out until you have paid the last penny."

~ MATTHEW 5:25-26

Jesus is all about healthy relationships. You hear that often in His teaching. Settle differences with people quickly and calmly. How? Swallow your pride and take the lead to talk things out.

You know that when you ignore problems they grow bigger and bigger, which will take a lot more time and energy to solve.

Take the high road, which is the road Jesus modeled, and settle your differences calmly.

Living it

Peace of conscience is nothing but the echo of pardoning mercy.

– William Gurnall

Forgiving Others

"If you refuse to forgive others, your Father will not forgive your sins."

~ MATTHEW 6:15 NLT

The bottom line of this statement is … don't ask for God's forgiveness if you aren't willing to forgive someone who has hurt you. Wow. That's scary. Where would you be without God's forgiveness? You don't want to sacrifice that, do you?

If you've ever just decided to ignore a person who has wronged you and felt pretty noble about it, like it is the Christian thing to do – you're wrong. Actually, the Christian thing to do is to forgive her. Totally, completely forgive her. Just as God forgives you, over and over and over.

Living it

Dear Father,
Forgive and forget, huh? That's what You want me to do. I always thought that forgiving was enough, but that it was alright to remember. Help me, Father. I can't do this without You. Help me to forgive *and* forget.

In Jesus' name, Amen.

How Spiritual Are You?

"When you fast, do not look somber as the hypocrites do, for they disfigure their faces to show others they are fasting. Truly I tell you, they have received their reward in full."
~ MATTHEW 6:16

Whose opinion of you is most important? God's or people's? Of course, your answer should be God's opinion. So, do a little self-check … are you "showy" about your faith? Do you wear the somber face of a spiritual giant? Do you make sure others know how sacrificially you give of your time? Do you pray aloud with beautiful but not heartfelt prayers? Why? So others will praise your spiritual level? Fine.

Jesus says that their praise is all the praise they will get. There will be no praise from God for public shows. Keep acts of service, giving and prayers private and personal – as much as possible just between you and God.

Living it

You must have the same attitude that Christ Jesus had. Though He was God, He did not think of equality with God as something to cling to. … He gave up His divine privileges; He took the humble position of a slave and was born as a human being. When He appeared in human form, He humbled Himself in obedience to God and died a criminal's death on a cross.
– Philippians 2:5-8 NLT

Between You and God

"When you fast, put oil on your head and wash your face, so that it will not be obvious to men that you are fasting, but only to your Father, who is unseen; and your Father, who sees what is done in secret, will reward you."

~ MATTHEW 6:17-18

*K*eep personal things personal. Some things should just be between you and God. For example, fasting should be a private thing. There's no need for everyone to know that you're fasting – especially by only looking at you.

Why does it matter? Because if you are concerned about what others think, then you aren't really focused on God and an act of faith like fasting should make you grow closer to Him, not to get attention from others.

Living it

Come, let us bow down in worship, let us kneel before the LORD our Maker; for He is our God and we are the people of His pasture, the flock under His care.

– Psalm 95:6-7

Learn to Trust

"Can any one of you by worrying add a single hour to your life?"

~ MATTHEW 6:27

It's so simple to say, "Don't worry. God is in control." Of course, you know that, but sometimes your heart or your mind just can't let go of some worry. Even when you give it to God, you keep grabbing it back.

Jesus knows that worry will suck the energy right out of your life. Worry takes away hope. Trust and worry cannot live in the same heart. There just isn't room for both. You can't change anything by worrying about it. Your worry won't lengthen your life; in fact it might shorten it. Learn to trust God; even if you must learn that by the tiniest of baby steps. Learn to trust.

Living it

Dear Father,
I don't *want* to worry. But, every time I give my worries to You, I end up snatching them back, just a little bit at a time. Sometimes You don't do things as quickly as I want You to. I'm sorry. Please forgive me and give me the courage to leave my worries with You.
In Jesus' name, Amen.

The Most Important Thing

"Do not worry, saying, 'What shall we eat?' or 'What shall we drink?' or 'What shall we wear?' For the pagans run after all these things, and your heavenly Father knows that you need them."

~ MATTHEW 6:31-32

Yes, God knows what you need. Does that mean you will always have everything you need? No, because there are lessons to be learned in times of need that can be learned no other way.

So what is Jesus saying here? There is a more important issue at stake than having exactly what you need – and that is a true, deep relationship with Jesus. Don't make "getting stuff" the thing that takes all your focus and your energy.

God knows what your needs are even before you know what they are. Stay close to Him and trust Him. That must be the most important thing.

Living it

In the darkest of nights cling to the assurance that God loves you, that He always has advice for you, a path that you can tread and a solution to your problem – and you will experience that which you believe. God never disappoints anyone who places his trust in Him.

– Basilea Schlink

What Do You Want?

"Seek first His kingdom and His righteousness, and all these things will be given to you as well."
~ MATTHEW 6:33

What do you want from God? His "stuff" such as His blessings and prayers answered and heaven someday, or do you want Him – His presence in your life?

Keep your eyes on what is important. Keep your eyes on the goal of knowing and serving Jesus. Ask Him to help your faith to grow stronger. Spend time with Him. Make Him the core of your everyday life and do not worry about anything. Yes, that's easy to say, but not so easy to do. That's OK. Life with God is a journey. Take it one step at a time.

Living it

But as for me, it is good to be near God. I have made the Sovereign LORD my refuge; I will tell of all Your deeds.
– Psalm 73:28

Taking Care of Business

"Hypocrite! First get rid of the log in your own eye; then you will see well enough to deal with the speck in your friend's eye."

~ MATTHEW 7:5 NLT

It's easy to criticize other people. You can so plainly see what they do wrong and how they need to improve their lives, so you might as well point it out to them, right? After all ... it's your responsibility, isn't it? Yeah, not so much.

Jesus said not to be critical of little things in someone else's life while willingly ignoring the big issues in your own life. Take care of your own business before you start criticizing someone else. If you look at yourself and others honestly, you may find that your actions are worse than theirs. Once you correct yourself you will be able to more clearly see how others need help, and be able to offer it in love.

Living it

Dear Father,

I look at my own life through rose-colored glasses that allows me to justify my own actions ... even if unfairly. Father, help me to be honest with myself. Reveal the "planks" in my own eyes. Help me to deal with those before I dare to criticize anyone else.

In Jesus' name, Amen.

Protect the Good Stuff

"Do not give dogs what is sacred; do not throw your pearls to pigs. If you do, they may trample them under their feet, and turn and tear you to pieces."

~ MATTHEW 7:6

Protect the valuable stuff. What is the most valuable thing you could give to another person? Your love and loyalty, of course. Jesus said to be careful where you place those things. If you give them to someone who isn't worthy of them, they will probably just trash them. They won't respect you, your love or your loyalty.

What Jesus is saying here is to give your heart and your loyalty to God, not people. Give valuable things to the One who deserves them and will treat them well: God.

Living it

Do you read this verse and think "yeah, yeah, whatever"? Do you feel that you do put God first and therefore your priorities are all in order? If you're correct – good for you. But before you decide that this verse doesn't speak to you, ask God to reveal any misplaced sacred things and see what happens.

God's Love Shown

"Which of you, if your son asks for bread, will give him a stone? Or if he asks for a fish, will give him a snake? If you, then, though you are evil, know how to give good gifts to your children, how much more will your Father in heaven give good gifts to those who ask Him!"

~ MATTHEW 7:9-11

You cannot begin to understand how very much God loves you. Jesus wants you to understand that. As much as you love your children, family and friends, and long to give them wonderful gifts, God loves you even more.

He will give you everything you need, and even things you don't need – blessings beyond anything you can ask or dream. Perhaps He doesn't always give what you "want," but that's because He knows what is best for you and because He knows what else is coming.

Living it

Every good and perfect gift is from above, coming down from the Father of the heavenly lights, who does not change like shifting shadows.

– James 1:17

How to Treat Others

> "So in everything, do to others what you would have them do to you, for this sums up the Law and the Prophets."
> ~ MATTHEW 7:12

It's so simple. Just treat others the way you would like to be treated. If everyone could do that it would ensure kindness, unselfishness, compassion, equality. It's the Jesus way of doing things.

It's too easy to get caught up in the "me-first attitude" of self-centeredness that makes you treat others badly. Jesus tells us not to do that. Treat others the way you would like them to treat you. If they aren't nice back, at least your conscience is clear. And who knows, they might just begin to treat you as nicely as you treat them!

Living it

We have committed the Golden Rule to memory; let us now commit it to life.
– Edwin Markham

Specific Choices

"Small is the gate and narrow the road that leads to life, and only a few find it."

~ MATTHEW 7:14

If God wants everyone to know Him, why does Jesus say this? Perhaps it is because no one accidentally slides into heaven or flies in hanging on someone else's coattail. Accepting Jesus is an intentional choice that every person must make. It will not always be the popular choice.

People who aren't interested in knowing Jesus travel a wide road, but it doesn't lead to a personal relationship with Him. Pay attention to Jesus and to God's Word and find the specific road that leads to life with Him.

Living it

Salvation is found in no one else, for there is no other name under heaven given to mankind by which we must be saved.

– Acts 4:12

Good Fruit/Bad Fruit

"Every good tree bears good fruit, but a bad tree bears bad fruit. A good tree cannot bear bad fruit, and a bad tree cannot bear good fruit."
~ MATTHEW 7:17-18

If you love Jesus and live in obedience to Him, that will show by how you live and how you share His love with others. If you don't love Him, that will eventually show in your life, too.

This is interesting, because some people will fool others into thinking that they are quite serious about Jesus. But they don't fool Jesus, and their lack of faith will eventually show in their life. Bear good fruit – learn to know Jesus better and better and give control of your life over to Him.

Living it

A tree is known by its fruit; a man by his deeds. A good deed is never lost; he who sows courtesy reaps friendship, and he who plants kindness gathers love.
– St. Basil

Truth Fruit

"By their fruit you will recognize them."

~ Matthew 7:20

Jesus followed His previous comment with this statement because there were people in His day (as there are today) who talk a good talk about knowing God. They talk about how they trust "the big guy upstairs" or call for prayer during a crisis.

But these people may not know God at all. How can you tell? Look at the "fruit" of their lives at a time when there is no crisis. If they have a consistent relationship with God, it will show. But if they only acknowledge God at a time of crisis or after a big victory – then maybe not.

Living it

Honesty time ... just between you and God. Look at the fruit of your life. What do you see? Yes, you love God and you do your best to obey Him. But is there fruit? Are the lives that you touch being influenced for Him?

The Real Thing

"On Judgment Day many will say to Me, 'Lord! Lord! We prophesied in Your name and cast out demons in Your name and performed many miracles in Your name.' But I will reply, 'I never knew you. Get away from Me, you who break God's laws.'"

~ MATTHEW 7:22-23 NLT

Some people were able to do things that would seem to only be possible with the power of God behind them. However, Satan and his demons can mimic some miracles. People might be fooled by these miracles, but Jesus makes it very clear that He is not fooled.

People who claim to do God's work but have not accepted Jesus as Savior are fakers. The day will come when they will hear these words: "Away from Me ..."

What does this mean to you? Be honest with Jesus. Accept Him and know Him. Don't try to impress others without the real thing in your heart.

Living it

How can we turn our knowledge *about* God into knowledge *of* God? The rule for doing this is simple but demanding. It is that we turn each Truth that we learn about God into matter for meditation before God, leading to prayer and praise to God.

– J. I. Packer

Deep Faith

"Everyone who hears these words of Mine and does not put them into practice is like a foolish man who built his house on sand. The rain came down, the streams rose, and the winds blew and beat against that house, and it fell with a great crash."

~ MATTHEW 7:26-27

How deep is your faith? Is it strong enough to trust Jesus through the really tough times in life? It's relatively easy to follow Him, claim His teachings and proclaim His love when your life is basically trouble free.

You learn how firm your foundation is when a job is lost, a relationship crumbles, your health falters ... whatever the problem.

If you've built a foundation of trusting God, believing His Word – regardless of what comes – then your faith will get you through and will grow deeper in the process.

Living it

Dear Father,

It's hard. When painful things come in life, it's just plain old hard. Sometimes my trust in You stands firm. But there are times when the difficulties seem to pile on top of the other and then, well, I have trouble. Forgive me. Help me. Strengthen me. Help my faith to grow.

In Jesus' name, Amen.

What Can You Do?

"The harvest is plentiful but the workers are few. Ask the Lord of the harvest, therefore, to send out workers into His harvest field."

~ Matthew 9:37-38

*T*he time is growing short. Jesus is coming back. The opportunity to accept Him will soon be gone. He wants people to know God personally and be sure of the promise of heaven.

There are still so many people who have not even heard of Jesus' sacrificial love; many would accept Him if they were just given the chance. Jesus asks you to pray for this work to be done. There is a part for you to play in this task. Ask God to show you what it is, equip you for it and give you the courage to do it.

Living it

We are therefore Christ's ambassadors, as though God were making His appeal through us. We implore you on Christ's behalf: Be reconciled to God.

– 2 Corinthians 5:20

Real Living

"Whoever finds their life will lose it, and whoever loses their life for My sake will find it."

~ MATTHEW 10:39

What an awesome statement! Losing your life – giving it to Jesus – doesn't take your life (your freedom, creativity or mind) away. No, giving control of your life to Jesus enriches your life and talents by giving real purpose, peace and joy.

Imagine waking up each day and knowing that your words and deeds will be used by God to make a difference in someone else's life. Yes, as Jesus says, your real life is found in living for Jesus and serving Him. A life with purpose – isn't that just awesome?

Living it

Set your minds on things above, not on earthly things. For you died, and your life is now hidden with Christ in God.

– Colossians 3:2-3

Simple, Trusting, Unquestioning Faith

"I praise You, Father, Lord of heaven and earth, because You have hidden these things from the wise and learned, and revealed them to little children. Yes, Father, for this is what You were pleased to do."
~ MATTHEW 11:25-26

The religious leaders of Jesus' day thought they knew everything. They thought they had all the answers about God and how to live for Him. They had a lot of head knowledge but apparently not much heart knowledge.

Jesus said that the simple faith of a child was more pleasing to God than the arrogance of the religious leaders. Because of that, those who have faith like little children understand more than those who think they have all the answers. Simple faith. Trusting faith. Unquestioning faith. This kind of faith pleases God.

Living it

Faith isn't the ability to believe long and far into the misty future. It's simply taking God at His Word and taking the next step.
– Joni Eareckson Tada

August

Rules ... or Mercy?

"If any of you has a sheep and it falls into a pit on the Sabbath, will you not take hold of it and lift it out? How much more valuable is a person than a sheep! Therefore it is lawful to do good on the Sabbath."

~ MATTHEW 12:11-12

The religious leaders criticized Jesus for helping a man on the Sabbath. They said that what He did was work, and work was prohibited on God's day. Really? Did they not understand that mercy is at the heart of all of Jesus' teaching? They said that the only way to follow God was to live by rules. Jesus didn't agree with that. He said that taking care of people is the way to show God's love.

Living it

Dear Father,
Thank You for the reminder that people are invaluable – and that showing love and compassion to them is more important than rules. Help me to "be Jesus" to those I meet each day.
In Jesus' name, Amen.

Careless Words

"I tell you that everyone will have to give account on the Day of Judgment for every empty word they have spoken."

~ MATTHEW 12:36

*C*areless words ... are they really a big deal? Yes, they are. Jesus says that one day you will answer for those words. Maybe you like to make your friends laugh at your humorous comments – you'll answer for those words. Maybe you're critical of others – you will answer for those, too. Maybe you have a quick temper that sends words flying out of your mouth before you think.

You say all kinds of things every day. Try to think before you speak – consider whether your humor is harming someone or if your criticism or temper is hurtful. Watch your words, because every one counts.

Living it

All kinds of animals, birds, reptiles and sea creatures are being tamed and have been tamed by mankind, but no human being can tame the tongue. It is a restless evil, full of deadly poison.

– James 3:7-8

Do You See and Hear?

"Blessed are your eyes, because they see; and your ears, because they hear."
~ MATTHEW 13:16 NLT

Look beneath the surface of this verse. Have you surrendered control of your life to Jesus so that you can actually see His presence in your life and hear His voice speaking words of guidance and love to you?

Seeing and hearing is spotty at best for those who struggle to give up control of their own lives. Seeing and hearing requires trusting and listening.

Living it

Dear Father,
I see ... sometimes. I hear ... once in a while. Neither happens as often as I'd like. I understand that I will not reach this level of communication with You until I really and truly trust You. I want to. Help me to trust You. Show me how.
In Jesus' name, Amen.

The Growing Kingdom

"The Kingdom of Heaven is like the yeast a woman used in making bread. Even though she put only a little yeast in three measures of flour, it permeated every part of the dough."

~ MATTHEW 13:33 NLT

Yeast changes things. When yeast is mixed into dough it spreads throughout and causes the dough to rise. Sometimes it seems as though the evil in this world is winning. It helps to remember that, like yeast, God's kingdom is steadily working its way into the hearts of people and spreading throughout the world. Yes, evil has a strong hold in the hearts of many. But one day, God's kingdom will prevail. Hold on to that hope.

Living it

Sometimes it does seem as though evil is winning. Take some time right now to list the ways that God's kingdom is growing. Note missionary work, progress in your city or neighborhood and especially in the lives of people around you. It's encouraging to remind yourself that God is still working!

Wheat and Weeds

"'No,' he answered, 'because while you are pulling the weeds, you may uproot the wheat with them. Let both grow together until the harvest. At that time I will tell the harvesters: First collect the weeds and tie them in bundles to be burned; then gather the wheat and bring it into my barn.'"

~ MATTHEW 13:29-30

Patience is a part of God's plan. Some people will choose to accept Jesus and follow Him. Those people are the "wheat" in this verse. People who choose not to accept Him are the "weeds." Both groups exist here on earth, but when the Day of Judgment comes (and it will) the "weeds" will not be allowed to enter heaven. By their own choice they have denied Jesus and will not spend forever with Him. As long as they remain on this earth there is the chance that they will change their minds and turn to Jesus. Pray for that.

Living it

The Bible promises us that Jesus will return to take His faithful followers with Him to live with Him in His glorious presence forever. Everyone else will be left behind to face God's wrath and judgment. If Jesus were to return today, do you know if He would take you with Him to heaven?

– Billy Graham

Caring for Basic Needs

"I have compassion for these people; they have already been with Me three days and have nothing to eat. I do not want to send them away hungry, or they may collapse on the way."

~ MATTHEW 15:32

Jesus cares about the basic needs of your life – even something as basic as whether or not you are hungry. How can you concentrate on listening to Jesus or growing in your faith if you are really, truly hungry?

Jesus wants those basic needs to be met. Of course there are hungry and thirsty people around the world today. Why doesn't He do something about that? He is – through His followers. How can you help?

Living it

I urge you, brothers and sisters, in view of God's mercy, to offer your bodies as a living sacrifice, holy and pleasing to God – this is your true and proper worship. Do not conform to the pattern of this world, but be transformed by the renewing of your mind. Then you will be able to test and approve what God's will is – His good, pleasing, and perfect will.

– Romans 12:1-2

For or Against

"Get away from Me, Satan! You are a dangerous trap to Me. You are seeing things merely from a human point of view, not from God's."

~ Matthew 16:23 NLT

Wouldn't it be devastating to hear Jesus say these words to you? They are powerful and Jesus said them to His friend Peter! Jesus had just predicted His own death ... part of the reason for Jesus coming to earth and Peter said, "No way! That won't happen."

Peter didn't understand the big picture of Jesus' purpose for coming into the world. He just didn't want anything bad to happen to his friend and master. But Jesus couldn't let anyone stand in the way – not Peter – not you – not anyone! This thought stands alongside the statement that you are either for Jesus or against Him. Work with Him to bring to pass the things of God.

Living it

Dear Father,

I've always identified with Peter because he seems so emotional. He doesn't always make the right choices, but he means well. Help me to measure my words, my thoughts, my reactions so that I always stand for You and let that show by my words and deeds.

In Jesus' name, Amen.

Give Up Control

"If any of you wants to be My follower, you must turn from your selfish ways, take up your cross, and follow Me."

~ MATTHEW 16:24 NLT

Giving up control is a daily, no, sometimes a minute-by-minute thing. But following Jesus means denying yourself – giving up control of what happens in your life and trusting Jesus – no matter what.

In this Scripture passage, Jesus had just told His disciples that He was going to die. He wanted His disciples to know that they must put aside their fear of suffering or pain and follow Him. Can you do that? It's important to stay focused on God's plan and follow Him ... come what may.

Living it

You may never know that Jesus is all you need, until Jesus is all you have.

– Corrie ten Boom

What's Most Important?

"What good will it be for someone to gain the whole world, yet forfeit their soul? Or what can anyone give in exchange for their soul?"

~ MATTHEW 16:26

Dear friend, what is most important to you? Do you dream of career success with power and wealth? Do you dream of expensive possessions? Do you simply dream of a loving family?

There's nothing wrong with any of those things except when they are chosen over knowing Jesus. In the big picture of eternity, what good is it to gain all of that stuff here on earth but to lose your soul to hell? Choose the most important thing – knowing God – and allow Him to lead the rest of your life.

Living it

God is not who you think He is; He is who He says He is.
– Clarice Fluitt

It's a Promise

"The Son of Man is going to come in His Father's glory with His angels, and then He will reward each person according to what they have done."

~ MATTHEW 16:27

It *is* going to happen. Jesus promised His followers that He would come back one day and take His followers to heaven with Him. What an amazing day that will be ... at least for some people. It will also be a day of facing how you have lived your life; what choices you made.

Jesus promises to reward you for your obedience to Him. But there will be no hiding or justifying your disobedience and no way to change it then. This is serious. Choose today to know, honor and obey Him.

Living it

As obedient children, do not conform to the evil desires you had when you lived in ignorance. But just as He who called you is holy, so be holy in all you do; for it is written: "Be holy, because I am holy."

– 1 Peter 1:14-16

Possibilities in Faith

"If you have faith as small as a mustard seed, you can say to this mountain, 'Move from here to there,' and it will move. Nothing will be impossible for you."

~ MATTHEW 17:20

Jesus was speaking to His disciples here. He wanted them to understand the possibilities of real faith. His followers could do amazing things if they truly, unquestioningly believed.

Think about the miracles Jesus did when He was on earth: healing people, raising the dead back to life, returning to life Himself. It is amazing to think about the possibilities when you believe without doubting and pray without questioning.

Living it

Dear Father,

I am certain I only access a small portion of the power available to me through You. Father, help my faith to grow. Help my walk with You to be more intimate so that Your power can flow through me and You can use me for Your purposes on earth.

In Jesus' name, Amen.

Humility vs. Pride

"Anyone who becomes as humble as this little child is the greatest in the Kingdom of Heaven."

~ MATTHEW 18:4 NLT

Jesus' teachings are counter to what your heart might say to you to be successful – at least if your heart listens to the media or much of what is written about success. Pride is at the other end of the spectrum from humility. Pride shouts, "Me, me!" Humility cares for others. A humble person thinks about others first and cares about what happens to them.

Jesus says that this kind of attitude is the winner in His kingdom. Children haven't learned the drive to be Number One and often you will find that they care about others' feelings and situations. Jesus instructs us to understand that life in His kingdom is not all about ourselves ... it's all about Him.

Living it

The smallest things become great when God requires them of us; they are small only in themselves; they are always great when they are done for God.

– François Fénelon

Money and Heaven

"How hard it is for the rich to enter the kingdom of God!"
~ MARK 10:23

Why? Why did Jesus say that it is hard for the rich to enter heaven? Maybe it's because some wealthy people won't give Jesus control of their lives. Maybe it's because some value their money more than anything else. Or maybe it's because some feel they don't need God since they can buy whatever they want.

Jesus wants His followers to know that money should be generously shared with others. Holding too tightly to material possessions or to control of your life makes it hard to serve God.

Living it

Dear Father,
It's a constant temptation to get sucked into the world's fascination with earning more and more money. But Father, I want to be focused on You and to stay dependent on You for everything. Help me to keep my focus on You and to know that You always meet my needs.
In Jesus' name, Amen.

Give Your Heart to God

"All things are possible with God."

~ MARK 10:27

Jesus made this statement in response to a question from His disciples as to who could be saved if rich people couldn't. They couldn't understand how the rich – who were so respected in society – couldn't get to heaven. But God can do anything – save anyone – help anyone – change anything.

God is God and nothing is impossible for Him! Therefore, if a rich person gives her heart to God, she will be saved. If any person gives her heart to God, she will be saved.

Living it

Where I found truth, there found I my God, who is the truth itself.

– St. Augustine

Turning Things Upside Down

"Whoever wants to become great among you must be your servant, and whoever wants to be first must be slave of all."
~ MARK 10:43-44

Does this sound like upside down thinking? Why would a person choose to be a servant or a slave? Most people dream of being the boss and being in control of others.

So why did Jesus make this statement? Simple: Remember that Jesus' teachings focus on loving others. That love is shown by putting others' needs before your own. So, in that sense you will be a servant to others instead of thinking of yourself first.

Living it

Christ Himself gave the apostles, the prophets, the evangelists, the pastors and teachers, to equip His people for works of service, so that the body of Christ may be built up until we all reach unity in the faith and in the knowledge of the Son of God and become mature, attaining to the whole measure of the fullness of Christ.

– Ephesians 4:11-13

God's Salt

"Salt is good, but if it loses its saltiness, how can you make it salty again? Have salt among yourselves, and be at peace with each other."

~ Mark 9:50

*A*re you a salt-o-holic? Do you just love salty food? Salt adds a lot of flavor, doesn't it? It changes the taste of food that is bland.

Jesus said that you are like salt to the people around you because you add flavor to living, taking the boring away. The flavor you add is the flavor of God's love and mercy. His love is deeper and stronger than anything and when you live for Him, you add that flavor to your relationships. You make a difference for God.

Living it

True Christians are to be in the world like SALT. Now salt has a peculiar taste of its own, utterly unlike anything else. When mingled with other substances, it preserves them from corruption. It imparts a portion of its taste to everything it is mixed with.

– J. C. Ryle

Servant Model

> "Even the Son of Man did not come to be served, but to serve, and to give His life as a ransom for many."
> ~ MARK 10:45

OK, think about it – Jesus is God's Son. He is the Creator. He is the Savior and yet He came to earth to serve. He thought about other people all the time. He thought about what He could teach them and what He could do for them. Others were His focus – not Himself.

Jesus calls for His followers to be servants in the same way, by putting others' needs and desires ahead of their own. Granted, it's not an easy thing to do. But, Jesus doesn't ask you to do anything that He didn't do Himself. He gave His time, energy and even His life for others.

Living it

Dear Father,
Thank You for sending Jesus to earth. He is my example. His life is a challenge to live in obedience to You. Thank You for that example. Thank You for Your Word that instructs me. Thank You for the Holy Spirit that strengthens and guides me.
In Jesus' name, Amen.

Faith

"Have faith in God."

~ MARK 11:22

It's simple – just have faith in God. Just believe and trust in God's power, strength and love – no matter what. Trust Him to take care of you and to protect you and guide you.

Sometimes God may seem to be a little silent, but if you truly have faith in God you will completely submit to Him because you know He is sovereign and that He loves you more than you can possibly imagine. Think how good life would be if you were to have complete faith in God.

Living it

Now faith is confidence in what we hope for and assurance about what we do not see.

– Hebrews 11:1

Do You Believe?

"Whatever you ask for in prayer, believe that you have received it, and it will be yours."

~ MARK 11:24

When you pray, do you really believe that God hears you and that He will answer? Prayer is such a privilege. It's your opportunity to tell God what's on your heart, what you are worried about, what you are hoping for, what you need.

Of course it is important to pray in God's will, which you can know by reading His Word and obeying Him. Then, the things you pray for will be in line with His will. It's wonderful that Jesus will hear your prayers and will answer them.

Living it

Pray continually.

– 1 Thessalonians 5:17

Be Honest

"Watch out for the teachers of the law. They like to walk around in flowing robes and be greeted with respect in the marketplaces, and have the most important seats in the synagogues and the places of honor at banquets."

~ MARK 12:38-39

It's a shame that Jesus had to warn people about the teachers of the law. They should have been the best at obeying God's law. They certainly knew the law well enough. They were the religious experts of their time, so they should be the ones whom people should respect and obey. But Jesus questioned their motives, because they wanted people to notice them – they felt that they were more important than other people.

Jesus sees a person's heart, so He knows why you do what you do. Be sure your motivations are pure and honest as you serve Jesus.

Living it

Time for a check-up ... what are your motivations? Do you want people to notice what you do? Do you seek power and authority? Make sure your motives are purely to serve Jesus and others – nothing more and nothing less.

Be Careful!

"Be on your guard; I have told you everything ahead of time."
~ MARK 13:23

Jesus thought of everything! He made sure that everything you need to know about living for God is in the Bible.

All the instructions and challenges you need to keep on track are there. But Jesus also warned us about people who might try to pull us away from God because they follow their own version of what the Bible teaches. Jesus said to be on the lookout for people who do not teach the truth. Be sure that you know what the Bible teaches and you will be just fine.

Living it

The Bible is not man's word about God, but God's word about man.
– John Barth

Future Hope

"Then everyone will see the Son of Man coming on the clouds with great power and glory. And He will send out His angels to gather His chosen ones from all over the world – from the farthest ends of the earth and heaven."

~ MARK 13:26-27 NLT

Life gets pretty difficult sometimes, right? It can be hard to find something positive to hold on to. You may even wonder where God is sometimes and why He doesn't seem to answer your prayers. There is one promise that Jesus made that gives bright hope for the future: you won't always be here on earth, mired in the difficulties of life. He is coming back!

Jesus was very clear about the future. He promised that He is coming back someday. He will return in great power and glory for the purpose of taking His children back to heaven with Him! Whatever problems you face in life will one day be history as you join Jesus in the glory of heaven forever!

Living it

Dear Father,
Thank You for the promise of eternity with You. That's a promise that gives me something wonderful to look forward to. It's incredible to think that I will be with You someday. Thank You for this indescribable gift.

In Jesus' name, Amen.

Don't Be Lazy

"Keep watch because you do not know when the owner of the house will come back – whether in the evening, or at midnight, or when the rooster crows, or at dawn. If he comes suddenly, do not let him find you sleeping."
~ MARK 13:35-37

Don't get lazy. Don't justify your actions or lifestyle by saying, "I'll live for Jesus later. Right now I want to have some fun." Jesus warns His followers to pay constant attention to how they are living, because no one knows exactly when Jesus will return to earth to bring His children to heaven.

Make the most of the time you have here to be effective in your work for Jesus. Be careful to constantly live for Him and be obedient to Him. Then you will be ready whenever He comes!

Living it

Dear Father,
I know I sometimes get lazy about realizing that Jesus' return could happen at any moment. I ask You to fill me with the urgency of sharing the gospel with others, because it could be any day.
In Jesus' name, Amen.

Worship with Abandon

"The poor you will always have with you, and you can help them any time you want. But you will not always have Me."

~ MARK 14:7

You probably know the story of the woman who poured some very expensive perfume on Jesus as she worshiped Him. She probably knew that people would criticize her for wasting the perfume, but she didn't let that stop her. She worshiped with abandon. She may have given the best of her possessions in her worship, holding nothing back.

Jesus received her worship and appreciated it. That's where this statement came in. He pointed out that the poor could be helped at any time, but her worship of Him was immediate. How can you worship with abandon? What "best" can you give?

Living it

It is in the process of being worshiped that God communicates His presence to men.

– C. S. Lewis

Keep On Fishing!

"Put out into deep water, and let down the nets for a catch."
~ Luke 5:4

Jesus made this statement to fishermen who had already been out fishing all night but had caught nothing. Peter wanted to argue with Jesus, probably because he was tired and discouraged. Instead, he did what Jesus asked and the result was a catch of fish so big that they could barely pull in the nets. Jesus blessed Peter beyond his wildest dreams because Peter believed Him and did what He asked.

Maybe you're tired and discouraged, too. Is it hard to get up every day and "keep dropping your nets into the water?" Don't give up – you never know when Jesus is going respond with a massive, wonderful blessing!

Living it

"I will send down showers in season; there will be showers of blessing."
– Ezekiel 34:26

Normal, Everyday People

"I have not come to call the righteous, but sinners to repentance."

~ LUKE 5:32

Jesus came for sinners. That's pretty much everyone, right? But what a comfort at times when you feel like all you do is mess up. There isn't anyone who is 100% righteous. Jesus knows that. He came for the normal everyday person who has good days and bad days, successes and failures.

God's plan from the minute Adam and Eve sinned was for Jesus to make a way for people to have a personal relationship with Him and to be forgiven of their sins. He will help you come face to face with your sin, so that you can repent. He loves you ... in your sin and through your sin.

Living it

Dear Father,

I'm so thankful for forgiveness. I'm so thankful that You care enough to forgive me over and over. Thank You for loving me through the good and the bad and for giving me second, third and fourth chances.

In Jesus' name, Amen.

Action

"Everyone who asks receives; the one who seeks finds; and to the one who knocks, the door will be opened."
~ Luke 11:10

How marvelous is this verse? God is waiting to hear from you. He cares about what you care about. He *wants* to answer your prayers. The key is: you must pray.

Does that mean you can ask for anything you want and be sure that you'll get it? Of course not – you must know God by reading His Word. The better you know Him, the more you will understand His will for your life. Keep praying to see God at work! The more you ask, the more you learn. The more you learn, the more you know.

Living it

Have you been praying for something for a very long time? Don't give up. God hears. He cares. He will answer in His time.

The Hardest Place

"I tell you the truth, no prophet is accepted in his hometown."

~ LUKE 4:24 NLT

This is one of the hardest things – the people you care about most are often the hardest to witness to. You don't want to be rejected by them. You don't want them to miss knowing Jesus so you might push hard.

Jesus knows how you feel. The people who knew Him best – the ones who watched Him grow from childhood to manhood – had trouble believing that He was God's Son. It's difficult to convince those closest to you because they know you the best. They know your bumps and bruises. Be patient and do your best to live your faith in front of them day in and day out.

Living it

Dear Father,

I'm sorry to admit that sometimes my behavior toward my family could be the exact thing that turns them away from You. O God, I love them so much and I want them to know You. Please help me to be a good example of a Christ-follower so that they will be drawn to You.

In Jesus' name, Amen.

Complete Submission

"Abba Father, everything is possible for You. Take this cup from Me. Yet not what I will, but what You will."
~ MARK 14:36

Jesus prayed this prayer in the Garden of Gethsemane. He knew that His arrest and death were coming. He knew it was going to be difficult. But He was completely submitted to God's plan. He gave everything.

Complete submission to God for you and me means surrendering completely to His will. It means trusting Him regardless of what His plan for you or your loved ones might bring. It requires a foundational belief in His true love for you.

Think about what Jesus faced after He prayed this prayer. That's true love that you can trust and should make the journey to complete submission easier.

Living it

The question in salvation is not whether Jesus is Lord, but whether we are submissive to His lordship.
– John MacArthur

Willing and Weak!

"Watch and pray so that you will not fall into temptation. The spirit is willing, but the flesh is weak."

~ MARK 14:38

Wow, did Jesus have this one right! Your spirit may want to obey and serve. Your spirit may want to honor the body and health God gave you. Your spirit may want to show love and kindness to all people around you. But sometimes your body can't keep up with your spirit and you stumble and give in to the temptation, turning away from those things your spirit wants to do.

Jesus tells us here to stay focused on Him. Watch and pray, because if you aren't focused, then no matter what your spirit longs for, you will fall into temptation. Remain focused on staying close to Jesus.

Living it

I do not understand what I do. For what I want to do I do not do, but what I hate I do. And if I do what I do not want to do, I agree that the law is good. As it is, it is no longer I myself who do it, but it is sin living in me.

– Romans 7:15-17

Absolutely Nothing

"My Father, who has given them to Me, is greater than all; no one can snatch them out of My Father's hand."
~ John 10:29

This statement does not mean that you will not have problems. It does not mean that you won't experience job loss or health issues or broken relationships. Those are all part of life. It does, however, mean that Jesus will walk beside you through whatever life brings your way. Nothing, absolutely nothing can change that.

Once you accept Jesus into your heart *you are His.* Hold on to that truth whatever comes your way.

Living it

Even when I walk through the darkest valley, I will not be afraid, for You are close beside me. Your rod and Your staff protect and comfort me.
– Psalm 23:4 NLT

September

You Are Not Alone

"Remain in Me, and I will remain in you. For a branch cannot produce fruit if it is severed from the vine, and you cannot be fruitful unless you remain in Me."

~ JOHN 15:4 NLT

The focus of this verse is often the command to stick close to Jesus because He is the source of strength and power. There's no doubt that it's good to have a reminder to do that. But look at the second part of that first sentence – He is sticking with you!

You're not alone. You don't have to do your work for Him on your own. You don't have to struggle through problems by yourself. Stick close to Jesus and He will remain with you.

Living it

You make known to me the path of life; You will fill me with joy in Your presence, with eternal pleasures at Your right hand.

– Psalm 16:11

A Close Relationship

"Anyone who does not remain in Me is thrown away like a useless branch and withers. Such branches are gathered into a pile to be burned."

~ JOHN 15:6 NLT

D on't take the command to "remain in Jesus" lightly. He means it. If you don't stick close to Him so that your purpose, power, energy and strength come from Him, then what use are you to Him? Yes, He does love you. But He has made it clear that He wants a close relationship with you. Don't ignore that.

Living it

Dear Father,

I want a close relationship with You, too. It should be easy to stick close to You, but it seems like something is always pulling me away. I don't understand. Please help me to remain in You and to grow my faith stronger and stronger.

In Jesus' name, Amen.

Completely Loved

"As the Father has loved Me, so have I loved you. Now remain in My love."
~ JOHN 15:9

Jesus loves you as much as His Father loves Him. Take a minute and think about that perfect love. It is a love so deep and so complete that you truly cannot fathom it. His love asks for nothing in return except that you love Him back and that you choose to stay close to Him. And that choice is such a blessing – it's a gift to yourself!

Living it

We know and rely on the love God has for us. God is love. Whoever lives in love lives in God, and God in them.
– 1 John 4:16

True Joy

"I have told you this so that My joy may be in you and that your joy may be complete."

~ JOHN 15:11

When Jesus was on earth He did a lot of teaching. But He wanted His hearers to know that He wasn't just giving them a bunch of rules. He knows that His teachings – the things you read in the Bible – will make your life better. They will improve your human relationships and help you to live closer to God. He loves you, so He wants your life to be filled with happiness – and being close to Him brings true joy.

Living it

Joy is a net of love by which you can catch souls.

– Mother Teresa

Love One Another

"My command is this: Love each other as I have loved you."
~ JOHN 15:12

This simple sentence packs a really big punch. Love as Jesus loves – unconditionally. Don't nitpick. Don't hold grudges. Give others the benefit of the doubt. Forgive when necessary. Just love.

Of course it isn't always easy to love this way, but you don't have to do it on your own. Jesus will help you to love others in ways you never knew you could. A life filled with love is so much better than a life filled with strife.

Living it

Dear Father,
I think I'm pretty good at loving others, but when I stop and think about it, I guess I get critical about some things. I'm sorry for that. I ask Your help to be more accepting and loving and to focus on the things that really matter.
In Jesus' name, Amen.

Looking for Proof

"Don't tell anyone, but go, show yourself to the priest and offer the sacrifices that Moses commanded for your cleansing, as a testimony to them."

~ LUKE 5:14

The hardest people to convince that Jesus was truly the Messiah – the Son of God – were the religious leaders. They thought they knew everything so they questioned pretty much everything Jesus said and did.

In this Scripture verse, He had just healed a man who had leprosy. He tells the man to keep quiet about it until he has told the priest and offered the sacrifices that were required. He wanted the man to do everything by the book so that the priest would have to admit that a miracle had taken place and that Jesus was the reason.

How willing are you to give Jesus credit for His work in your life? Do you question everything or simply say, "Thank You"?

Living it

If the only prayer you ever say in your entire life is "thank you," it will be enough.

– Meister Eckhart

Treat Others Fairly

"Do not judge, and you will not be judged. Do not condemn, and you will not be condemned. Forgive, and you will be forgiven."

~ LUKE 6:37

Treat other people the way you want to be treated. That shouldn't be difficult. Unfortunately it sometimes is.

This command must be important, because Jesus made this point a couple of times. It's important to treat other people the way you want to be treated, He said, by other people and by God. You want fair judgment, second chances, forgiveness? Then give those same things to others. Think about how you treat others because it matters.

Living it

I have decided to stick with love. Hate is too great a burden to bear.

– Martin Luther King, Jr.

Follow the Leader?

"Can the blind lead the blind? Will they not both fall into a pit?"

~ Luke 6:39

This makes so much sense. If you find yourself emulating someone or getting close enough that your footsteps and behavior match, be sure that leader is a Christ-follower.

If you choose to follow someone who doesn't follow Christ, don't expect to grow stronger in faith and service. It will be, like Jesus says, the blind leading the blind. If you listen to someone who doesn't really know any more than you know (even if she acts like she does), then you aren't going to get good guidance and help.

Be careful who you follow. In fact, follow only Christ – that's the safest option.

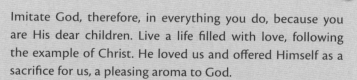

Living it

Imitate God, therefore, in everything you do, because you are His dear children. Live a life filled with love, following the example of Christ. He loved us and offered Himself as a sacrifice for us, a pleasing aroma to God.

– Ephesians 5:1-2 NLT

Look in the Mirror

"Why do you look at the speck of sawdust in your brother's eye and pay no attention to the plank in your own eye?"
~ LUKE 6:41

Self-preservation is a natural reaction to life. But sometimes it can make you critical of others, while justifying your own problems.

No one is perfect; every single person is a sinner. So why judge someone for some small fault you see in them when there are huge problems in your own behavior? Look in the mirror and see what's wrong in your own life. Don't worry about others. God will take care of them!

Living it

Dear Father,
Reveal my own weaknesses to me. I know I ignore them or justify them, but I really want to know. God, help me to deal with my own issues instead of criticizing others.
In Jesus' name, Amen.

Generous Hearts

"Give to everyone who asks you, and if anyone takes what belongs to you, do not demand it back."

~ Luke 6:30

Jesus asks you to be focused on others. He wants people to take care of one another. That means giving, helping and serving, while expecting and asking nothing in return.

If Jesus had His way, no one would go hungry and no one would be homeless, because those who had food and money would share with the poor.

Have you ever helped someone, either anonymously or expecting nothing in return? It feels so good, doesn't it? When knowledge of your generosity is between just you and God, it is true service to Him.

Living it

We can do no great things, only small things with great love.

– Mother Teresa

What's Inside Counts

"No good tree bears bad fruit, nor does a bad tree bear good fruit."

~ LUKE 6:43

*W*hat's in your heart will eventually show in your life. If you live your life for Jesus, it will be apparent by the kindness and concern you show for others. That will be the good fruit you bear.

If you live for Jesus, it will be impossible for you to bear bad fruit, like selfishness, unkindness or a lack of compassion. People will be able to see that Jesus is in your heart by the way you live.

Living it

Wherever a man turns he can find someone who needs him.
– Albert Schweitzer

Pruning

"He cuts off every branch in me that bears no fruit, while every branch that does bear fruit He prunes so that it will be even more fruitful."

~ JOHN 15:2

Pruning a tree or bush means cutting back the branches quite heavily. It may not look good at the time, but it's good for the plant. It will make the plant healthier in the long run, because it gets rid of unhealthy branches that use food and water and may be growing the wrong way.

God prunes your life, too. It can be painful, but Jesus promises that some of the difficult times are actually to help you grow stronger in your relationship with Him. It can be difficult, but stay focused on what you can learn from your hardship.

Living it

Are you going through difficulties right now? Are you tired and perhaps discouraged that God isn't solving your problems? Could it be that these situations are God's work of pruning away the things that shouldn't be in your life? Or perhaps they are pruning away your lack of trust in Him?

Loving Obedience

"If you keep My commands, you will remain in My love, just as I have kept My Father's commands and remain in His love."
~ JOHN 15:10

Jesus made it very clear: Obeying Him is key to your relationship with Him. Of course, no one can obey all the time, because people have sinful hearts. But Jesus looks at whether your heart's desire is to obey Him, even when you don't. When you obey or desire to obey, you can be confident of God's love.

What does obeying mean? It is serving God with honesty and unselfishness; caring for others and doing whatever work God puts before you.

Living it

The LORD will again delight in you and make you prosperous if you obey the LORD your God and keep His commands and decrees that are written in this Book of the Law and turn to the LORD your God with all your heart and with all your soul.
– Deuteronomy 30:9-10

Laying Down Your Life

"Greater love has no one than this: to lay down one's life for one's friends."

~ JOHN 15:13

What does this mean? Do you have to die for someone in order to show your love? Actually, there are other ways of laying down your life for another person. You may lay down your life by giving sacrificially of your time or money to help another person.

When you give your life to God in full-time service, that is laying down your life to show your love for others and for God. How do you lay down your life for others and for God?

Living it

Only when we give joyfully, without hesitation or thought of gain, can we truly know what love means.

– Leo Buscaglia

Real Friendship

"I no longer call you servants, because a servant does not know his master's business. Instead, I have called you friends, for everything that I learned from My Father I have made known to you."

~ JOHN 15:15

Jesus is your friend and you are His. What does that mean on a personal level? A friend cares about what you're dealing with and willingly shares your load. A friend comes alongside you without even being asked. A friend celebrates your victories because she cares.

Just as you call your best friend to share news, Jesus also shares news with you. He shares everything He learned from His Father. He wants you to know how to please God and how to live for Him. Jesus loves you so much. How awesome is that?

Living it

Look at the relationship described in this verse. Jesus takes your relationship with Him from the master/servant level to a friendship. A servant only knows information that her master chooses to share. A servant does what she is told to do. A friend knows personal information. A friend is more of an equal. Jesus wants a close relationship with you – a friendship.

Stop Striving

"Why do you worry about clothes? See how the flowers of the field grow. They do not labor or spin. Yet I tell you that not even Solomon in all his splendor was dressed like one of these."

~ MATTHEW 6:28-29

You just can't outdo God. You can do everything in your power to take care of yourself, provide for yourself and promote yourself ... but God does it all better than you can.

If you need proof of that, look around at the amazing world He created. It's gorgeous. It's got something for everyone. He did it all and He will give you everything you need to live. So stop striving and stop worrying and just let God take care of you.

Living it

Praise the LORD. Blessed are those who fear the LORD, who find great delight in His commands.

– Psalm 112:1

Watch Out for Wolves

"Watch out for false prophets. They come to you in sheep's clothing, but inwardly they are ferocious wolves."
~ MATTHEW 7:15

People who teach things that go against what the Bible says can make their way sound so wonderful and right. They appear to really care about the people around them, but in reality they are concerned only with themselves. Jesus calls such people ferocious wolves disguised in sheep's clothing.

Pay attention to the things you are taught. Measure them against Scripture and ensure your teachers are giving the entire Scripture, not just parts of it that they have manipulated to fit their own purposes.

Living it

Jesus warns against listening to people who teach things that don't agree with what He teaches. Some people think they know the right way, but if you look at how they live their lives you see that their lives do not reflect Jesus or His love. Often they have taken only parts of Jesus' teaching to obey instead of the whole Bible. Their goal may be only to promote themselves or gain financially from their followers. Be careful.

Good Thoughts

"Why do you entertain evil thoughts in your hearts?"

~ MATTHEW 9:4

Have you ever had an argument with your husband or a friend – only the person you were arguing with knew nothing about the disagreement? You know how it goes: you get upset about something and let it roll around in your mind and heart – having private arguments in your mind and always winning those arguments.

When evil, selfish thoughts come into your mind, push them out. Keep pleasant and fair thoughts in your heart. Think about things that make you a better person and more loving and helpful to others.

Living it

Whatever is true, whatever is noble, whatever is right, whatever is pure, whatever is lovely, whatever is admirable – if anything is excellent or praiseworthy – think about such things.

– Philippians 4:8

Taking a Gentle Stand

"Whoever acknowledges Me before others, I will also acknowledge before My Father in heaven."
~ MATTHEW 10:32

Don't expect Jesus to claim you if you don't claim Him.

It is a part of a Christian's honor to be able to share the love of God with other people. The openness of your faith, which spills out of a heart devoted to God, shows God's love to others.

Jesus honors this faith by acknowledging you to God as one of His own. It's not always easy to let the people around you know that you are a Christian, especially your family members. Do so gently and with respect, showing them the love that Jesus has shown you.

Living it

Dear Father,

This is so scary to me. I'm kind of nervous about sharing my faith with my family. I long for them to know You, but I also do not want them to be angry with me or avoid me. Show me how to gently and patiently share my faith with them. Prepare their hearts, O God, and give me wisdom.

In Jesus' name, Amen.

The Holy Spirit

"The Advocate, the Holy Spirit, whom the Father will send in My name, will teach you all things and will remind you of everything I have said to you."

~ JOHN 14:26

The Holy Spirit is Jesus' amazing gift to believers. The Spirit lives in your heart, so He's always with you. You are never, ever alone. The Spirit guides and teaches you how to live for God and how to know Him better.

That still, small voice or the little push in your heart that you sometimes feel is quite likely the Spirit leading you to make good choices. He even prays for you when you can't find the words to express yourself. God sent His Spirit to be with believers because He loves you very much.

Living it

You also were included in Christ when you heard the message of truth, the gospel of your salvation. When you believed, you were marked in Him with a seal, the promised Holy Spirit, who is a deposit guaranteeing our inheritance until the redemption of those who are God's possession – to the praise of His glory.

– Ephesians 1:13-14

Part of the Process

"Come, follow Me," Jesus said, "and I will send you out to fish for people."
~ Matthew 4:19

Jesus always knew why He was on earth. He never lost His focus about what His job was. You have a job, too. When you gave your life to Jesus you acquired a new purpose in life. You now have the same purpose He has – to bring people to faith in Him. As you follow Jesus, He will show you how to be a part of the process of leading others to faith in Him.

Jesus used the fishing example in talking with His disciples because they were fishermen. Look for Him to use in ways you are familiar with also. Maybe you will be the first step of developing a friendship with someone and then another believer will take things from there. Jesus will use your strengths and the gifts God gave you.

Living it

Dear Father,
I'm excited and honored to be a part of Your work on earth. I pray for opportunities to share Your love with others. And, if I don't have chances to verbally share, help me to remember that I'm always sharing You by the way I live and by how I treat others. May my life leave a sweet scent that draws others to You!
In Jesus' name, Amen.

The Heart of Jesus

"Blessed are the poor in spirit, for theirs is the kingdom of heaven."

~ MATTHEW 5:3

The world gives a great deal of recognition to powerful, strong and wealthy people. But Jesus made it plain that none of those things are most important to God.

Jesus gives honor to those who are poor in spirit. That doesn't mean financially poor people. It means those who are humble and who show kindness, respect and honor to others. That's the kind of spirit that reflects the heart of Jesus.

Living it

Treat everyone with politeness, even those who are rude to you – not because they are nice, but because you are.

– Anonymous

Heavenly Rewards

"Rejoice and be glad, because great is your reward in heaven, for in the same way they persecuted the prophets who were before you."
~ Matthew 5:12

Be happy that someone is giving you a hard time? Rejoice if you are actually being persecuted? Is Jesus serious? Yes, He is.

This is a "big picture" statement. Jesus is reminding you that doing God's work is the most important thing. You may meet with resistance and even anger by living for Christ or witnessing for Him, but that's OK because you are pleasing God and you will be rewarded in heaven. He knows what's happening and He will reward His faithful followers.

Living it

Consider it pure joy, my brothers and sisters, whenever you face trials of many kinds, because you know that the testing of your faith produces perseverance.

– James 1:2-3

Go the Extra Mile

"If anyone forces you to go one mile, go with them two miles."

~ MATTHEW 5:41

What's your reaction when someone "makes" you do something? Do you get defensive and resentful? Do you resist anyone else having control over your time and energy? Jesus says not to do that. He even says to go the extra mile. So, whatever is asked of you, do that and even more.

Surprise people with your generosity, helpfulness and kindness. And make sure they know that it comes from a heart focused on loving and obeying Jesus.

Living it

Dear Father,

It seems like this verse was spoken just for me. I'm sometimes so resentful when my schedule is interrupted. Help me to get over myself. Help me to be willing to go the extra mile in a way that shows love and compassion and generosity.

In Jesus' name, Amen.

A Generous Heart

"Give to those who ask, and don't turn away from those who want to borrow."

~ MATTHEW 5:42 NLT

Scripture warns us to be careful with our resources – to be a good steward of what we have.

But a woman with a generous heart sees a need and, as she is able, she meets that need without worrying whether it's tax deductible or if anyone knows of her good deed.

A generous heart is an unselfish heart, which is what Jesus encourages. Don't hold on to your possessions as though they are more important than people. Be generous to all, and do not worry about being repaid.

Living it

No man is more cheated than the selfish man.

– Henry Ward Beecher

Growing Faith

"You of little faith, why are you so afraid?"

~ MATTHEW 8:26

The disciples were scared because they were in a boat and a storm blew up. They were afraid that the boat would sink. After all they had been through with Jesus you might think they would have faith that He would protect them. They knew He could do anything! However, they were human and sometimes they were scared that Jesus wasn't going to take care of them.

Maybe you feel the same way sometimes. When you think about it, it must have made Jesus sad that His disciples' faith wasn't stronger since they knew so much about Him. But He didn't give up on them, and He won't give up on you either. Just ask Jesus to help your faith grow stronger and you will see that happening a little bit at a time.

Living it

"I do believe; help me overcome my unbelief!"

– Mark 9:24

Desperate Prayers

"Take heart, daughter," He said, "your faith has healed you."
~ MATTHEW 9:22

A woman who had been sick for twelve years be-lieved that just touching the hem of Jesus' robe would heal her. That is amazingly strong faith. Jesus recognized it and rewarded it.

There is a key word here: "faith". When problems arise, many people start praying for God to fix every-thing. They may be surprised when He doesn't answer their prayers. Spouting a prayer when life gets tough, but having no relationship with Jesus before or after that prayer is not faith in action. It is desperation.

Faith is what healed the woman Jesus was speaking to here – not desperation. Go and do likewise.

Living it

In the gospel the righteousness from God is revealed, a righ-teousness that is by faith from first to last, just as it is written: "The righteous will live by faith."

– Romans 1:17

Day In and Day Out

"As you go, proclaim this message: 'The kingdom of heaven has come near.'"

~ MATTHEW 10:7

Life can sometimes feel like you are doing the same old thing day in and day out. It may even be oppressive at times.

Jesus' statement reminds you that in everyday living you should keep your focus in mind – sharing the message of God's love with those around you. There will be opportunities in how you live, how you speak and how you act to show others the love of God.

Living it

Dear Father,

Life is pretty constant and it feels like one day is the same as the next. Help me to remember that the living I'm doing is also the time of influence I have for You. People are watching me to see You. May they see Your love through my words and deeds.

In Jesus' name, Amen.

Submit

"It will not be you speaking, but the Spirit of your Father speaking through you."
~ MATTHEW 10:20

Jesus sent His disciples out to begin experiencing ministry on their own. It might have been scary for them – after all, most of them were just ordinary men: fishermen or tax collectors.

Jesus reminded them that the Spirit was with them and if they would be submitted to Him, He would do the speaking for them. Does that give you comfort in your own life? Don't stress over ministering for God; submit to the Spirit and let Him use you.

Living it

There will be times when people attack your faith and you simply won't know how to defend yourself or God. Jesus said to stay super close to God and to rely on the Holy Spirit in those times. He will give you the right words to speak. He will help you to be courageous but respectful, strong but kind, and His words will actually be the words of God, spoken through your lips!

In or Out?

"Whoever disowns Me before others, I will disown before My Father in heaven."

~ MATTHEW 10:33

One day you will stand before the judgment seat of Christ, as all believers will. This is serious business. Jesus warns people not to take their relationship with Him lightly. If you try to stay on the fence; not committing but not denying your belief in Jesus, you can be sure the day will come when you will have to take a stand.

If you deny Jesus because you're too embarrassed or scared of what others might think of you, then don't expect Him to stick up for you, either. Get in or get out – there is no riding the fence here.

Living it

You will not stroll into Christlikeness with your hands in your pockets, shoving the door open with a careless shoulder. This is no hobby for one's leisure moments, taken up at intervals when we have nothing much to do ... It takes all one's strength, and all one's heart, and all one's mind, and all one's soul, given freely and recklessly and without restraint.

– A. J. Gossip

October

Bearing Witness

"Go back to John and tell Him what you have heard and seen – the blind see, the lame walk, the lepers are cured, the deaf hear, the dead are raised to life, and the Good News is being preached to the poor."

~ MATTHEW 11:4-5

*A*n eyewitness testifies of what she has seen or heard and that is often the deciding voice in a court case. As a witness of Jesus' work you can testify of His power and love so that others may believe in Him. Jesus told people around Him to do just that. It's also a way for you to share Him with others – and to encourage yourself along the way as you give an account of what He's doing in your life.

Living it

That last sentence may be significant – what *is* He doing in your life? Do you see God doing anything, or are you walking so far from Him that His presence is not apparent? Get close. Be still. Listen and watch. Then you will see what you can share.

Critical Words

"You brood of vipers, how can you who are evil say anything good? For the mouth speaks what the heart is full of."

~ MATTHEW 12:34

Jesus had just cast a demon out of a man, yet the Pharisees criticized Him. They claimed He got His power from Satan! Their critical words came from hearts that were filled with anger, fear and jealousy.

The emotions you are harboring in your heart will eventually show in the words you speak. They will come out eventually. In Psalms David asked God to search his heart and to make it clean. Everyone needs to ask God to do that once in a while.

Living it

The LORD said to Samuel, "Do not consider his appearance or his height, for I have rejected him. The LORD does not look at the things people look at. People look at the outward appearance, but the LORD looks at the heart."

– 1 Samuel 16:7

Family Ties

"Whoever does the will of My Father in heaven is My brother and sister and mother."
~ Matthew 12:50

There is no doubt that Jesus loved His mother and brothers. He talked about love all the time. But, can you see the importance of this statement? Those who obey God and do what He instructs are closer than actual family.

Remember, though, that it isn't just "doing" that makes you family of Jesus. It is also "being", which means resting in Him and trusting Him – really knowing Him.

Living it

Dear Father,
I understand that just reading Your Word and even praying to You isn't enough. I long to "be" with You ... to sense Your spirit dwelling in me. I long to be so extravagantly Yours that my thoughts and actions flow naturally in a way that honors You.
In Jesus' name, Amen.

Understanding

"The knowledge of the secrets of the kingdom of heaven has been given to you, but not to them."

~ MATTHEW 13:11

Jesus had just told a story about seeds being planted. Some of the people who heard the story couldn't figure out what the message was. Jesus drew His disciples aside and explained. In a sense, He pulled aside the curtains so they could see what was on the other side.

You have that same viewpoint because of the totality of Scripture. Jesus trusts you with the secrets of heaven. Don't take that lightly. Read them. Learn them. Know them.

Living it

When a Christian shuns fellowship with other Christians, the devil smiles. When he stops studying the Bible, the devil laughs. When he stops praying, the devil shouts for joy.

– Corrie ten Boom

Closed Hearts

"For the hearts of these people are hardened, and their ears cannot hear, and they have closed their eyes – so their eyes cannot see, and their ears cannot hear, and their hearts cannot understand, and they cannot turn to Me and let Me heal them."

~ MATTHEW 13:15 NLT

Developing a calloused heart is a choice. It often happens through disappointment, pain or anger. A person allows her heart to grow a thick, hard-to-penetrate shell. She will not be touched by the truth of God's Word and sometimes does not even care for other people. It's a sad condition because it keeps her apart from God.

But, it isn't hopeless because she could choose to open her heart to Jesus. He would heal that calloused heart so she could live in His love.

How's your heart? Is it open to Jesus or calloused and closed?

Living it

Dear Father,
I've closed my heart to You in some areas. I know it. I was disappointed. I was hurt. I didn't understand. Now my heart is calloused and I don't know how to fix it. Heal my heart, dear Lord, soften it and speak Your love into it. Thank You.
In Jesus' name, Amen.

Holding Nothing Back

"Whoever wants to save their life will lose it, but whoever loses their life for Me will find it."

~ MATTHEW 16:25

Some things in life you must do all the way – you can't "sort of give birth," you can't "sort of lose weight successfully." And, you can't "sort of follow Jesus." You are either in or you're out.

Complete surrender means giving your wants, hopes, dreams, time, activities and passions to Jesus. It means obeying Him by learning what He wants you to do and how He wants you to live. It means holding nothing back. It's a day-by-day journey of growth – not always easy, but it comes with the promise of His presence in your life and the knowledge that you will have eternity with Him!

Living it

The wisdom that comes from heaven is first of all pure; then peace-loving, considerate, submissive, full of mercy and good fruit, impartial and sincere.

– James 3:17

Dazzling Faith

"Truly I tell you, unless you change and become like little children, you will never enter the kingdom of heaven."
~ MATTHEW 18:3

When a little girl or boy gets excited about something – from princesses to super heroes – it consumes their young mind and becomes all they talk about. Their playtime is focused on it and their "Will you get it for me?" begging is focused on it.

Wow. Are you that excited about your faith in Jesus? Are you consumed with love for Him? Are your thoughts filled with Him? Maybe that consuming, dazzling kind of faith is what Jesus meant here. Get excited about Jesus.

Living it

Remember those first days of following Jesus? You were excited. You were consumed with learning and growing. Has your faith grown a little subdued and habitual, weighed down by the busyness of life? Let your heart recapture that excitement and amazement that you have a personal relationship with God!

Influential Living

"Woe to the world because of the things that cause people to stumble! Such things must come, but woe to the person through whom they come!"

~ MATTHEW 18:7

When you open a brand-new loaf of bread and find that the first piece is moldy, you may flip through and find that several more slices have been affected by that mold. It spreads its influence.

In much the same way, people spread their influence to others and sometimes lead people into sin. Jesus' words encourage you to think about the influence you have on those around you. Influence people toward, not away from Him.

Living it

If I can put one touch of a rosy sunset into the life of any man or woman, I shall feel that I have worked with God.

– George MacDonald

Never Alone

"In the same way your Father in heaven is not willing that any of these little ones should perish."
~ MATTHEW 18:14

Children didn't have much place in the hierarchy of society in Jesus' day. But in this instance, Jesus pulled a small child into the room and explained that just as a shepherd would leave ninety-nine sheep on a hillside to go and find one sheep that had wandered away, God desires for all His children to stay close to Him. He pays attention to you and to where you are in your journey of knowing Him. So, you can know that you aren't alone and He hasn't turned away. He cares. A lot.

Living it

It is by grace you have been saved, through faith – and this is not from yourselves, it is the gift of God – not by works, so that no one can boast.
– Ephesians 2:8-9

Prayer Partners

"I also tell you this: If two of you agree here on earth concerning anything you ask, My Father in heaven will do it for you."

~ MATTHEW 18:19 NLT

Prayer partners are a good thing. Praying with a friend gives accountability that you aren't trying to manipulate God. Praying together gives comfort that someone else understands what concerns you and what is on your heart. It builds a bond between two Christian women.

Does this verse mean that God will always do exactly what you ask? Of course not. God sees a much bigger picture than you can. It does mean that there is power and blessing in praying with one another.

Living it

Nothing tends more to cement the hearts of Christians than praying together. Never do they love one another so well as when they witness the outpouring of each other's hearts in prayer.

– Charles Finney

Don't Go It Alone!

"Where two or three gather in My name, there am I with them."

~ MATTHEW 18:20

Togetherness. Relationships. Connections. Jesus is all about these things. It's safe to say that the Christian life is not intended to be lived apart from others. Join with people of similar beliefs and passions in prayer, worship and service to God.

Remember Ecclesiastes 4:9-10 that, just like the verse above, reminds us of the strength in numbers. One person can accomplish some things, but a group of people can encourage one another and help one another to accomplish so much more!

Living it

Two people are better off than one, for they can help each other succeed. If one person falls, the other can reach out and help. But someone who falls alone is in real trouble.

– Ecclesiastes 4:9-10 NLT

Forgiveness for All

"I tell you, not seven times, but seventy-seven times."

~ MATTHEW 18:22

Forgiveness is not always easy, especially when the offender doesn't believe she needs forgiveness. But the thing about anger and grudges is that they hurt only the one who is holding on to them – not the person they're angry towards. So, forgive and forgive and forgive, because it's better for you.

When you think about it – it's also what Jesus does for you. Don't keep score with how much you are forgiving, just do it. Forgiveness and restoring the relationship is the point.

Living it

Dear Father,
Forgiveness is not easy for me. It's more natural for me to hold grudges, but I know that isn't right. Help me to be willing to forgive, just as I hope others will forgive me. Fill me with Your forgiveness and love toward those who hurt me.

In Jesus' name, Amen.

Forgive Yourself

"The servant's master took pity on him, canceled the debt and let him go."
~ MATTHEW 18:27

*T*he man Jesus referred to in this story had a hopelessly large debt. There was no way he'd ever be able to repay it.

Imagine how he felt when the king forgave his debt – just wiped it off the books. He had asked for the king's patience and promised to pay back every cent. But the king had mercy on him and canceled the debt completely and let him go!

True forgiveness forgets as well as forgives. This is what Jesus does with your sin. He doesn't just forgive, He forgets, too. Then you should also forgive yourself. Don't hold on to guilt for something God has forgiven.

Living it

I can forgive, but I cannot forget, is only another way of saying, I will not forgive. Forgiveness ought to be like a canceled note – torn in two, and burned up, so that it never can be shown against one.

– Henry Ward Beecher

Forgive as You Are Forgiven

"Shouldn't you have had mercy on your fellow servant just as I had on you?"

~ MATTHEW 18:33

In continuing the story of the man who had been forgiven a huge debt, Jesus said that the man had another man thrown in jail because of a small debt the man owed him. Where is the justice in that? Since the man received grace for a big debt, why didn't he offer the other man grace for a small debt?

What's the message? Forgive as you have been forgiven. Sure, there will be times when others wrong you and hurt you; sometimes on purpose, sometimes not. What is to be your response? Plain and simple ... just forgive.

Living it

To be a Christian means to forgive the inexcusable, because God has forgiven the inexcusable in you.

– C. S. Lewis

Let It Go

"This is how My heavenly Father will treat each of you unless you forgive your brother or sister from your heart."
~ MATTHEW 18:35

Jesus ended His story of forgiveness with a warning. Don't take this lesson lightly because there is a penalty for refusing to forgive others. God notices that selfishness and it appears that it is useless to ask God to forgive you if you refuse to truly and honestly forgive others.

Are you holding on to some anger and hurt? It's tiring to hold so tightly to those feelings, isn't it? Let it go. Forgive ... and be forgiven.

Living it

Dear Father,
Help me to forgive and forget. I understand that I should not ask forgiveness from You if I'm not willing to forgive others. You don't hold grudges against me, so help me to let go of grudges against others. Help me to forgive and love as You love.
In Jesus' name, Amen.

The Heart's Understanding

"Why do you ask Me about what is good?" Jesus replied. "There is only One who is good. If you want to enter life, keep the commandments."

~ MATTHEW 19:17

A rich man asked Jesus how to find eternal life. The answer: obey the commandments. But, not only that, recognize the greatness and goodness of God. Give Him the respect, honor and worship He commands! Because of that recognition, you will obey the commandments God has given. What's in your heart will be lived out in obedience.

Living it

Your words may speak of loving and honoring God. Perhaps you speak of His sovereignty and power. But does your life prove that you believe the words you speak? Are you obeying or justifying? Are you loving or judging?

How You Treat Others

"'You must not murder. You must not commit adultery. You must not steal. You must not testify falsely.'"
~ MATTHEW 19:18 NLT

A wealthy man asked Jesus which commandments he had to obey in order to receive eternal life. Jesus mentioned six – the six that involve how others are treated. Much of Jesus' teaching focused on the two relationships of life: the vertical – between God and you; and the horizontal – between you and other people.

Why did He focus on these particular commands here? Probably because what's in a person's heart will show in how she treats others. If you truly love and obey God, it will show in your daily life through care, compassion and generosity.

Living it

It's interesting that Jesus mentions the commandments about relating to other people rather than the ones that focus on how to relate to God. He knew that face-to-face relationships could be harder to maintain than a spiritual relationship with Christ. It's important to have healthy relationships with others.

Hold Nothing Back

"If you want to be perfect, go, sell your possessions and give to the poor, and you will have treasure in heaven. Then come, follow Me."

~ MATTHEW 19:21

A rich man declared that he had obeyed the six commandments that Jesus pointed out in the previous verse. So, just to prove His point, Jesus challenged him on the topic that he knew the man held closest to his heart – his wealth. The man couldn't give up his wealth so he walked away.

Jesus asks you to give Him your all. He knows what you hold back from Him. Have you given your all to Jesus, or are you holding something back from Him? What are you afraid of? Do you trust Him completely?

Living it

In everything I did, I showed you that by this kind of hard work we must help the weak, remembering the words the Lord Jesus Himself said: "It is more blessed to give than to receive."

– Acts 20:35

No Second Place

"I tell you the truth, it is very hard for a rich person to enter the Kingdom of Heaven."

~ MATTHEW 19:23 NLT

Some people have a sort of prosperity theology, which says that God's blessings have been given to the wealthy. So, why would Jesus make this statement? Wealthy people are often powerful and some may feel that since they can buy whatever they want, they have no need of God. People scurry to please them, serve them and be close to them. Jesus says in this verse that they may put the value of their wealth ahead of their devotion and submission to God. What they don't realize is He plays second place to no one.

Living it

You must worship no other gods, for the LORD, whose very name is Jealous, is a God who is jealous about His relationship with you.

– Exodus 34:14 NLT

The First Shall Be Last

3e3

"Many who are first will be last, and many who are last will be first."

~ MATTHEW 19:30

The first shall be last. What is Jesus saying here? *Powerful, famous, influential, wealthy.* These are all words that describe people who are used to being first. They are used to being respected, honored and getting their way. They sometimes lord their power over "less important" people.

They expect respect and privilege from those who are poorer, quieter, more humble, self-sacrificing and concerned for others – those who are not as powerful or famous. But when it comes to God's kingdom, this last group will be first because of their dependence on God and concern for others. Where are you in this spectrum? First or last?

Living it

Listen, my dear brothers and sisters: Has not God chosen those who are poor in the eyes of the world to be rich in faith and to inherit the kingdom He promised those who love Him?

– James 2:5

Power of Faith

"Truly I tell you, if you have faith and do not doubt, not only can you do what was done to the fig tree, but also you can say to this mountain, 'Go, throw yourself into the sea,' and it will be done."

~ MATTHEW 21:21

How strong is your faith? Do you believe deep in the core of your heart that Jesus can and *will* answer your prayers? Of course, this great faith is guided by God's will and purposes. You can't ask that a mountain be thrown into the sea just for fun.

Jesus rewards faith that is focused on His purposes; faith that accepts His answers and still presses on regardless of disappointment. Faith that trusts Jesus completely has great power.

Living it

Faith is two empty hands held open to receive all of the Lord.

– Alan Redpath

Rules, Rules, Rules

"You must be careful to do everything they tell you. But do not do what they do, for they do not practice what they preach. They tie up heavy, cumbersome loads and put them on other people's shoulders, but they themselves are not willing to lift a finger to move them."

~ MATTHEW 23:3-4

People are what matter. Not rules. Jesus' warning is that some folks get so caught up in keeping rules that they lose compassion and concern for people.

Of course rules that are God's commands are important, but the Pharisees of Jesus' day interpreted those commands in their own stringent way – and left out the commands to care for others. Remember what's important and find a balance in obedience and love.

Living it

Biblical orthodoxy without compassion is surely the ugliest thing in the world.

– Francis Schaeffer

Who Are You Trying to Impress?

"Everything they do is for show ..."
~ MATTHEW 23:5 NLT

*W*hy do you do what you do? Assuming you are a Christ-follower, do you join Bible studies, work in refugee ministries, teach Sunday school, pray aloud in groups ... whatever you do, why do you do it?

Do your actions come from a heart devoted to serving God? Do your actions come from a need for others to see you and admire your very spiritual behavior? Don't "serve God" for the praise and admiration of others; do it because you love God completely.

Living it

Dear Father,
Search my heart. Show me, Father, if I'm doing things for the wrong reason. I think I'm just serving You, but if there are underlying motives, reveal them to me so that my service may be pure.
In Jesus' name, Amen.

Misplaced Honors

"Do not call anyone on earth 'father,' for you have one Father, and He is in heaven."

~ MATTHEW 23:9

It's OK to admire other people and to respect their knowledge or their spiritual walk. But don't forget that God is the supreme Authority in the world. He is your Father. He is your Guide. He will not share those positions of honor with anyone or anything else. Respect, worship and love Him.

No one should ever be equal with God in your heart. When someone else is there, there is always the danger of being led away from the truths of Scripture.

Living it

There is nothing so abominable in the eyes of God and of men as idolatry, whereby men render to the creature that honor which is due only to the Creator.

– Blaise Pascal

Know the Truth

"Watch out that no one deceives you."
~ MATTHEW 24:4

Sometimes people do not even realize they are deceiving others by their teachings because they are deceived themselves. Jesus' warning is to measure the things you are taught against the truth of Scripture. If something goes against Scripture then you know it isn't true. Be careful to not be led away from the truth. Of course, you can only do this by staying in God's Word and knowing it yourself.

Ask God to open your eyes to the truth taught there and to help those truths settle firmly in your heart.

Living it

Work hard so you can present yourself to God and receive His approval. Be a good worker, one who does not need to be ashamed and who correctly explains the Word of Truth.
– 2 Timothy 2:15 NLT

Wait in Expectation

"About that day or hour no one knows, not even the angels in heaven, nor the Son, but only the Father."

~ MATTHEW 24:36

Jesus is coming back! He promised He would come to take His children to heaven. No one knows when that will happen, but you should always be ready. Just like having your suitcase packed and waiting by the door for your airport ride to come, so you should keep your heart ready for Jesus to come.

Live in obedience to Him. Stay close to Him by reading His Word, praying and meditating. Be ready to meet Him at any moment. Wait in expectation!

Living it

We ought to be living as if Jesus died yesterday, rose this morning, and is coming back this afternoon.

– Adrian Rogers

Laying Up Treasures in Heaven

> "Then the King will say to those on His right, 'Come, you who are blessed by My Father; take your inheritance, the kingdom prepared for you since the creation of the world.'"
> ~ MATTHEW 25:34

*E*ver since the beginning of the world – the days of creation – God has been preparing your home in heaven. He's waiting for you. How awesome is that?

Jesus promises that He will come back to earth one day and take you to heaven. You will receive the rewards of how you've lived for Him – "laying up treasures in heaven." But the greatest reward of all will be living forever in His presence. Isn't that amazing?

Living it

Dear Father,
This is hard to even imagine – that I can actually be in Your heaven with You. What a gift. What an honor. What grace. Thank You for Jesus' sacrifice. Thank You for Your love.
In Jesus' name, Amen.

Caring for Others

"I was hungry and you gave Me something to eat, I was thirsty and you gave Me something to drink, I was a stranger and you invited Me in, I needed clothes and you clothed Me, I was sick and you looked after Me, I was in prison and you came to visit Me."

~ Matthew 25:35-36

There are so many people in this world who have so little. There are millions who would like to have what you toss out each day. Jesus' description of a person who lives by His principles is that of a person who cares for the poor and needy. She pays attention, giving to and helping those whom society would consider undesirable or outcast. By showing care and concern for these people, you will be showing it for Jesus.

Living it

This is a daunting idea when you consider how to care for people on your own. But there are many organizations that have ministries in place to care for those who have so little and need so much. Do you know of them? Are you helping them and praying for them?

Loving Others

"The King will reply, 'Truly I tell you, whatever you did for one of the least of these brothers and sisters of Mine, you did for Me.'"
~ MATTHEW 25:40

Hungry, naked, sick and imprisoned. Those are the people Jesus said His followers should help. Wherever you live you will find people like this. You may even find established ministries working with them. Jesus said, plain and simple, that helping these kinds of people is helping Him.

Remember that He said that to "love your neighbor as yourself" is the second greatest commandment. What would you do if you were one of these people? What would you want someone to do for you? Good. Then go and do that.

Living it

Dear Father,
I care. I just haven't known what to do and, OK, I admit it, I'm concerned about giving away money that I need to care for my own family. Father, break my heart for these needs that break Yours. Open my heart and show me how I can help.
In Jesus' name, Amen.

Choose ... and Live

"Who would patch old clothing with new cloth? For the new patch would shrink and rip away from the old cloth, leaving an even bigger tear than before."

~ MARK 2:21 NLT

The things Jesus taught didn't mesh with things the religious leaders of His day taught. He seemed like a sort of revolutionary. He knew that, too. So He warned people that it wasn't wise to weave what He taught into the fabric of the old things they had been taught.

For today, that means you shouldn't try to combine your old way of life with the teachings of Scripture. You must choose one or the other. Jesus' way is life, love, hope and promise. Choose that way today.

Living it

As for God, His way is perfect; the LORD's Word is flawless; He shields all who take refuge in Him.

– 2 Samuel 22:31

More Understanding

"With the measure you use, it will be measured to you – and even more."
~ MARK 4:24

Do you wish that you understood Scripture more deeply? Or that you more fully knew what Christ's plans for you are? The essence of this statement is that the more you listen and understand Scripture, the more understanding He will give you.

As you understand Scripture, its truth will show in your life. The way you accept others will show the truth of God's Word. Begin to accept the truths of Scripture, in faith, and the more you begin to see, the more He will reveal to you.

It's a journey in faith and you may take two steps forward and one step back, but keep pressing forward, as you grow and understand more and more of living life for Jesus.

Living it

Dear Father,
I think I understand Scripture, but maybe I don't let it sink into my heart so that it changes the way I live. Help me to be like a sponge, soaking up Your truths and living them out every day.
In Jesus' name, Amen.

November

What's It Going to Take?

"Why are you so afraid? Do you still have no faith?"
~ MARK 4:40

What does Jesus have to do to get you to trust Him? He must have wondered that as He saw His own disciples' faith faltering. They had seen Him do miracles. They had heard Him teach. They had asked Him questions ... but they still didn't fully believe.

You've seen Him do miracles, too. You've experienced His protection, provision and care. You've got the Scriptures to read and learn from. You have the testimonies of other believers. But the bottom line comes down to what's in your heart.

Do you trust Him? If you do, your fears will fade away. If you don't, your fears will push everything else out of your heart. Is He worthy of your trust? Then do not be afraid.

Living it

Jesus asked His disciples the above question after He had calmed a storm on the sea. He had just performed an amazing miracle – the weather did what He told it to do! They had seen Him do other miracles before this, but they still didn't trust Him enough to keep them from being afraid. He must have wondered what else He had to do or say to earn their trust. Would He ask you this same question?

Rules vs. Love

"You have a fine way of setting aside the commands of God in order to observe your own traditions!"

~ MARK 7:9

This sounds like a compliment, but it isn't. Jesus had simply had it with people who made up their own rules about how to live the Christian life.

People sometimes add to what Scripture teaches or they conveniently leave some aspect of His teaching out. Or, in extreme cases, they make up whole new rules! Whatever they do, it's wrong that they categorize others by these rules.

Jesus tell us not to draw lines in the sand and declare things like, "If you do *this* then you're Christian. If you don't do *this* then you're not." Just love people. Let God take care of their obedience.

Living it

Love is like a beautiful flower which I may not touch, but whose fragrance makes the garden a place of delight just the same.

– Helen Keller

Heart Choices

"From within, out of a person's heart, come evil thoughts, sexual immorality, theft, murder, adultery, greed, wickedness, deceit, lustful desires, envy, slander, pride, and foolishness. All these vile things come from within; they are what defile you."
~ MARK 7:21-23 NLT

It's kind of scary when you realize that sin isn't just the things you do – sin starts in your heart. Initially the decision on what you do or say begins with a choice made in your heart. Once the choice is made, the action will follow.

How's your heart today? Focused on Jesus? Eager to know, serve and obey Him? Whatever is in your heart is soon going to show to everyone else by your actions.

Living it

Let the message of Christ dwell in you richly as you teach and admonish one another with all wisdom through psalms, hymns, and songs from the Spirit, singing to God with gratitude in your hearts. And whatever you do, whether in word or deed, do it all in the name of the Lord Jesus, giving thanks to God the Father through Him.
– Colossians 3:16-17

Compassion in Practice

"I have compassion for these people; they have already been with Me three days and have nothing to eat."

~ MARK 8:2

Thousands of people were gathered to hear Jesus preach. He had been teaching for three days. He knew, though, that they couldn't continue to listen and learn since they were hungry. He cared about the fact that they needed food.

Jesus wanted their physical as well as their spiritual needs met. Pretty cool, huh? He had compassion for practical needs. He asks His followers to have the same kind of compassion for others. Meet practical needs as well as spiritual needs in those around you.

Living it

Finally, all of you, be like-minded, be sympathetic, love one another, be compassionate and humble. Do not repay evil with evil or insult with insult. On the contrary, repay evil with blessing, because to this you were called so that you may inherit a blessing.

– 1 Peter 3:8-9

Who Do You Say He Is?

"Who do people say I am? … But what about you?" He asked. "Who do you say I am?"

~ MARK 8:27, 29

Jesus asked Peter, one of His closest followers, what the word on the street was about Him. He had done all kinds of miracles in God's name. He had taught about God and how to live for Him; now He wondered if people were getting it. Did they believe that He was God's Son, the Messiah, who came to save the world?

A couple of verses later Jesus asks Peter who he thinks Jesus is. It's an individual belief. You don't get to heaven by grabbing onto the coattails of another believer. Who do you say Jesus is?

Living it

Take some time and think about this question, "Who do you say Jesus is?" You know the "right" answer and you can give it. Perhaps in your mind you believe it, but do you believe it in your heart? Do you believe strongly enough that Jesus is the Christ that it shows in your life?

Denying Self

"Whoever wants to be My disciple must deny themselves and take up their cross and follow Me."

~ Mark 8:34

W hat does it mean to deny yourself? Following Jesus means submitting or surrendering to His will. It means giving up your desires to do whatever Christ wants for you.

Taking up your cross means being faithful to Him no matter how tough life gets ... even when you don't want to do the things He asks of you, even when you're tired. It's not easy sometimes, but it is always worth it because your faith grows stronger with each step.

Living it

Brokenness is the shattering of my self-will – the absolute surrender of my will to the will of God. It is saying "Yes, Lord" – no resistance, no chafing, no stubbornness – simply submitting myself to His direction and will in my life.

– Nancy Leigh DeMoss

What Is Real Life?

"Whoever wants to save their life will lose it, but whoever loses their life for Me and for the gospel will save it."
~ MARK 8:35

Do you have control issues? Do you sometimes fight Jesus over how you spend your time, what choices you make or trusting Him with your loved ones? Does it feel like giving up control over your own life means you are losing your life?

There is no doubt that it's sometimes scary. But, remember that Jesus loves you more than you can imagine. So giving up control to Jesus delivers you from the hopelessness of a life without His guidance and love. Giving your life to Jesus actually implants purpose and direction in your life.

Living it

It is wonderful what miracles God works in wills that are utterly surrendered to Him. He turns hard things into easy, and bitter things into sweet. It is not that He puts easy things in the place of the hard, but He actually changes the hard thing into an easy one.

– Hannah Whitall Smith

Caring for All

"Whoever welcomes one of these little children in My name welcomes Me; and whoever welcomes Me does not welcome Me but the One who sent Me."

~ MARK 9:37

Children didn't hold much importance to adults in Jesus' day. The most important were healthy, wealthy men ... except where Jesus was concerned. Jesus cared about those who were unimportant to others and He wanted His followers to do the same.

Think about the people you show love and concern for. Are you going out of your way to care for those who society has overlooked?

Living it

Dear Father,

I guess if I think about new people in the neighborhood or visitors to our church, I realize that I do overlook some people. This is mostly because I'm shy, but that doesn't make it right. Give me courage to reach out to people and to see the opportunity for new friendships.

In Jesus' name, Amen.

Childlike Faith

"I tell you the truth, anyone who doesn't receive the Kingdom of God like a child will never enter it."
~ MARK 10:15 NLT

What attributes of a child is Jesus talking about here? Children are eager to learn, are sincere and are totally dependent on someone else for their livelihood and care. There is no pride in a child who is dependent upon another person to provide for her and care for her. Hopefully there is humility in recognizing her need.

Can you come before Christ with that same humble attitude? Eager, sincere and totally dependent on Him for everything? Let go of control. Let go of pride. Trust Him. Just trust Him.

Living it

Dear Father,
I think I can be totally dependent on You for my own life. It's harder, though, to trust You completely with people I love. I care so much and while I know You care, too, I guess I want You to act more quickly sometimes. I'm sorry for my lack of belief. Help me to trust You completely.
In Jesus' name, Amen.

Keeping the Commandments

"You know the commandments: 'You shall not murder, you shall not commit adultery, you shall not steal, you shall not give false testimony, you shall not defraud, honor your father and mother.'"

~ MARK 10:19

A rich man asked Jesus how to know that he would have eternal life. There were no special rules for the wealthy. Jesus asked the man how he treated others. Was he kind, fair and moral? Did he treat others with the respect and honor they deserved?

There are no shortcuts to eternity. It matters to Jesus how people treat one another. Love for God is shown not just by how you treat Him, but also by how you treat others.

Living it

We know and rely on the love God has for us. God is love. Whoever lives in love lives in God, and God in them.

– 1 John 4:16

Pray. Wait. Trust

Jesus looked at them intently and said, "Humanly speaking, it is impossible. But not with God. Everything is possible with God."

~ MARK 10:27 NLT

Do you really believe this? Jesus said that *nothing* is impossible for God. This is wonderful because it's a reminder that not a single one of your problems or concerns are too big for Him. You can be sure that He can handle any prayer request you have.

Never give up on God – He can do anything! Bring your requests to Him. Patiently wait for Him to act and then trust His answers.

Living it

Great is our Lord and mighty in power; His understanding has no limit.

– Psalm 147:5

Give All to Jesus

"Truly I tell you," Jesus replied, "no one who has left home or brothers or sisters or mother or father or children or fields for Me and the gospel will fail to receive a hundred times as much in this present age ... And in the age to come eternal life."

~ MARK 10:29-30

Do you have to leave all your loved ones behind to follow Jesus? Not necessarily, but you must reorder your priorities so that Jesus is always first. That means trusting Him to care for them and submitting to whatever His choices are.

What do you get in return? The blessings of knowing and serving Him, which means the peace, joy and assurance that you are loved; His purpose in your life; the assurance that your prayers are heard; and the wonderful promise of eternal life. These blessings are too great to even count.

Living it

Dear Father,
This is hard. I love my family fiercely. I wish to love You more fiercely. I want You to be Number One and own my heart completely. I can say that because I trust You totally with my loved ones. Your love is complete.

In Jesus' name, Amen.

God's Word

"Heaven and earth will pass away, but My words will never pass away."
~ MARK 13:31

God's Word is a gift. God has protected it through centuries of persecution so that it is available to His children. In it is what He wants you to know about Him and His care for you. In it you can read the history of how He interacted with and cared for His children.

Jesus promises that God's Word will never be lost. No matter what else happens, God's Word will survive ... for you and for generations to follow. Make reading it and meditating on it a part of your daily habits so that you will come to know God better and better.

Living it

Do you treasure God's Word? Do you long to read it? Do you read it over and over as you do a letter from a dear loved one? Don't take it for granted. God has done a lot through the centuries to make sure it's available to you in a form you can understand. Read it and learn from it.

Worship Matters

"Truly I tell you, wherever the gospel is preached throughout the world, what she [the woman with the alabaster jar] has done will also be told, in memory of her."

~ MARK 14:9

$\mathcal{A}$ woman – not a religious leader, a nobody in the eyes of the men around Jesus – took expensive, fragrant perfume and anointed Jesus with it. She worshiped Jesus through her actions.

There were men there who had heard the same news – that Jesus was going to die, but they did nothing. Jesus knew that she understood His message and she was worshiping Him. What she did was so important that it was recorded in the Bible and people are still talking about her thousands of years later. Never doubt that your worship matters to Jesus.

Living it

Sing to the LORD a new song; sing to the LORD, all the earth. Sing to LORD, praise His name; proclaim His salvation day after day. Declare His glory among the nations, His marvelous deeds among all peoples. For great is the LORD and most worthy of praise.

– Psalm 96:1-4

He's Coming Back

"I am," said Jesus. "And you will see the Son of Man sitting at the right hand of the Mighty One and coming on the clouds of heaven."

~ MARK 14:62

Jesus had kept silent through two rounds of His ridiculous trial. Then in the final session when they couldn't find any crime with which to convict Him, a religious leader point-blank asked Jesus if He was the Messiah. Jesus' answer was, "I am." He knew the man asking Him the question was not a friend, but Jesus pointedly answered that He was indeed God's Son, the Messiah. So He was declared guilty of blasphemy.

Except ... He was telling the truth, and not only that, He said that He would one day come back to earth. He's coming. Be ready.

Living it

Dear Father,

I can't imagine what that night was like for Jesus. I'm completely humbled to realize that He went through that whole night ... for me. The words "thank You" are not enough for me to utter. I worship You, and I eagerly anticipate Jesus' return. In Jesus' name, Amen.

One Way

"Whoever believes and is baptized will be saved, but whoever does not believe will be condemned."

~ MARK 16:16

There is one way to heaven. That's it. Only one way. Regardless of those who teach other pathways, Jesus says the only way is to believe in Him. The choice is a personal one, so each person must make her own choice about believing.

You must make the choice. You can't sit on the fence and expect salvation – go through the gate and leave the fence behind. Make a choice for Jesus. The person who does not believe is not saved and will not ever be invited into heaven.

Living it

The greatest enemy to human souls is the self-righteous spirit which makes men look to themselves for salvation.

– Charles Spurgeon

Straightened Priorities

"It is written: 'Man shall not live on bread alone.'"
~ LUKE 4:4

Taking care of physical needs is a priority, especially if there is a danger of those needs not being met. If you struggle with knowing where your next meal is coming from, then you will be thinking about that meal a lot. Satan tempted Jesus to turn away from God and honor Satan. Jesus didn't do it, of course. But you learn some interesting things during this experience.

One is to stop thinking about your physical needs ... whether you're hungry, cold, poor, rich, or whatever. This is hard if you're truly starving. But Jesus seems to be saying not to give up on Him in the face of hunger or other hardship. Make staying close to Him the most important thing.

Living it

Dear Father,
Help me to separate my "needs" from my "wants." Sometimes I lose focus on You because my needs and wants get mixed up. Then I get discouraged that You aren't answering my prayers. Oh, Father, help me to trust You with my needs. Help me to know that You always are taking care of me.
In Jesus' name, Amen.

Humble Hearts

"Blessed are you who are poor, for yours is the kingdom of God."

~ LUKE 6:20

Is Jesus saying that the Kingdom is only for the poor? We know that one other time He said it is hard for a rich person to enter heaven. It may be that money has nothing to do with it – what comes with wealth may be the key.

You need to be humble and dependent on God. Jesus lived an example of this kind of humility – serving others, helping people who were seen as unimportant and doing what God wanted Him to do. A humble heart is welcomed into the kingdom of God.

Living it

God is not looking for extraordinary characters as His instruments, but He is looking for humble instruments through whom He can be honored throughout the ages.

– A. B. Simpson

What Do You Hunger For?

"Blessed are you who hunger now, for you will be satisfied."
~ LUKE 6:21

Everyone hungers for something. What do you hunger for? Marriage? Friendship? Wealth? Power? What is it that races through your mind in the middle of the night, creating a longing that makes you yearn?

Jesus said that if you hunger for the right things, you will be satisfied. Wanting to know God better, serving Him more fully, being more obedient to Him ... that's what will make you feel satisfied and fulfilled.

Living it

I want to know Christ and experience the mighty power that raised Him from the dead. I want to suffer with Him, sharing in His death, so that one way or another I will experience the resurrection from the dead!

– Philippians 3:10-11 NLT

Blessed Obedience

"Blessed are you when people hate you, when they exclude you and insult you and reject your name as evil, because of the Son of Man."

~ LUKE 6:22

You've probably read stories of missionaries and Christians around the world who have been martyred for their faith in Christ. You may never face that kind of persecution. But you may find that some people will not be kind to you because you follow Jesus. Your obedience to God makes them uncomfortable and they may show that by rude comments or worse.

That's OK. You will be blessed for your obedience to Christ ... by Jesus Himself!

Living it

Dear Father,

Give me the courage and strength to stand firm for You. I've never faced real persecution, but I pray for the inner courage to not be afraid, should it come. I pray for the courage to proclaim Your name each and every day.

In Jesus' name, Amen.

Serve God or Money

"What sorrow awaits you who are rich, for you have your only happiness now."
~ LUKE 6:24 NLT

Money has become a god for some people. In our society today no one ever has enough. There is always a striving for more. The more they have, the more they want. Sure, they share some of their money. The sad thing is that so much of their focus is on getting more money and then on investing their money and protecting it. Life becomes all about money.

What's missed because of this? Often it's time with loved ones: simple time, doing simple things. They also miss serving, loving and obeying God. Jesus says that if money is your focus ... money is all you're going to get.

Living it

If a person gets his attitude toward money straight, it will help straighten out almost every other area in his life.
– Billy Graham

Spiritual Poverty

"Woe to you who are well fed now, for you will go hungry. Woe to you who laugh now, for you will mourn and weep."

~ Luke 6:25

Jesus is still talking about wealthy people here. Wealth often blinds people to their spiritual poverty – the need to be saved.

The old saying that money can't buy happiness is certainly true when it comes to salvation. You can't buy your way into heaven either – no matter how generous you are with your wealth. Salvation is only through belief in Jesus and a heart humbled before Him.

Living it

Do not think me mad. It is not to make money that I believe a Christian should live. The noblest thing a man can do is, just humbly to receive, and then go amongst others and give.

– David Livingstone

A Good Student

"The student is not above the teacher, but everyone who is fully trained will be like their teacher."

~ LUKE 6:40

A student who studies under a favorite teacher will often adopt that teacher's viewpoints and beliefs. Who is your teacher? Are you focused on studying God's Word and becoming more and more like Jesus?

You can't learn to be like Jesus apart from Him and you will never know more about living for God than He does. So, it makes sense to study the Bible and stay as close to God as you can. Learn from the Master Teacher.

Living it

My goal is that they may be encouraged in heart and united in love, so that they may have the full riches of complete understanding, in order that they may know the mystery of God, namely, Christ, in whom are hidden all the treasures of wisdom and knowledge.

– Colossians 2:2-3

Good Heart

"Each tree is recognized by its own fruit. People do not pick figs from thornbushes, or grapes from briers."

~ LUKE 6:44

What's in your heart comes out in your behavior and words. Maybe you've struggled to "be" Christian in a certain situation, but you caved in to behavior that didn't honor Christ. The attitudes in your heart will come out in your life eventually.

Jesus' example of a tree having fruit of a certain kind reveals that a heart devoted to Him will show love and kindness to people and God's creation. A heart that doesn't know God cannot be expected to show love and concern for others. Keep your heart focused on God and your "fruit" will honor Him.

Living it

Dear Father,
Sigh ... I do struggle with living out what I say I believe. I yearn for my "fruit" to be honorable to You. I long for my life to draw others to You. Free me of myself, Father, and help me to be submissive to Your will for my life.

In Jesus' name, Amen.

The Firmest Foundation

"I will show you what it's like when someone comes to Me, listens to My teaching, and then follows it. It is like a person building a house who digs deep and lays the foundation on solid rock. When the floodwaters rise and break against that house, it stands firm because it is well built."

~ LUKE 6:47-48 NLT

The foundation you build on matters. If your faith in Jesus is not your own – if you've followed Him because it seemed like the popular thing to do, your foundation is no good. Perhaps the decision to follow Him was yours, but you've not made any effort to grow in knowledge and strength, then your foundation is still shaky.

To stand firm, build a good foundation by getting to know God's Word, and learn to trust Jesus with small things and big things. Then, whatever storms come your way, you will stand firm with Him.

Living it

Since, then, you have been raised with Christ, set your hearts on things above, where Christ is, seated at the right hand of God. Set your minds on things above, not on earthly things.
– Colossians 3:1-2

No Hopelessness

"Your faith has saved you; go in peace."

~ LUKE 7:50

Jesus spoke these words to a woman who could understandably have been hopeless. She had two strikes against her – everyone knew she had lived a sinful life, and she was a woman: two difficult things to overcome in her day.

Still, she courageously came to Jesus when He was surrounded by a group of men and she worshiped Him. Her faith in Jesus saved her, and with it the promise of a life of peace. No sin, no situation is too big for Jesus to handle. If you believe in Him, you can trust Him completely.

Living it

Faith is a bird that feels dawn breaking and sings while it is still dark.

– Rabindranath Tagore

Necessary Faith

"The knowledge of the secrets of the kingdom of God has been given to you, but to others I speak in parables, so that, 'though seeing, they may not see; though hearing, they may not understand.'"

~ LUKE 8:10

The depth of understanding needed to grow a stronger relationship with Jesus only comes through faith, which reveals the deeper meaning of His words. Over and over again Jesus stresses how important faith is.

If you don't believe Jesus is God's Son and that He came to earth to teach about the only way to know God, was killed and rose back to life, then the true message of His teaching will make no sense to you. It will be like hearing someone speak a language you don't understand. Jesus' message is for His followers.

Living it

Who is it that overcomes the world? Only the one who believes that Jesus is the Son of God.

– 1 John 5:5

Light in Darkness

"No one lights a lamp and hides it in a clay jar or puts it under a bed. Instead, they put it on a stand, so that those who come in can see the light."

~ LUKE 8:16

You have the light inside you – the light of God's love and power. What are you doing with it? Ignoring it so it flickers faintly? Hiding it so no one will see it? What good is a light that is hidden?

The purpose of light is to break through darkness and reveal what is hidden by that darkness. Jesus called Himself the Light of the World and when you asked Jesus to be your Savior, His light came into your life. You became one more point of light for Him in a world filled with the darkness of sin.

Living it

Dear Father,
I want my light to shine brightly so that all who know me may see You. Help me, Father, to consistently, surely, shine for You.
In Jesus' name, Amen.

No Secrets

"There is nothing hidden that will not be disclosed, and nothing concealed that will not be known or brought out into the open."

~ LUKE 8:17

*A*braham Lincoln once said, "You can fool some of the people all of the time, and all of the people some of the time, but you cannot fool all of the people all of the time."

There's another element of that – you can't fool God *any* of the time. He knows and sees everything. Everything is revealed to Him and eventually you will have to answer to Him for the choices you have made. So, the best thing to do is not keep secrets. Come clean, confess what you need to confess and repent.

Living it

If we claim to be without sin, we deceive ourselves and the truth is not in us. If we confess our sins, He is faithful and just and will forgive us our sins and purify us from all unrighteousness.

– 1 John 1:8-9

Good Listening

"Pay attention to how you hear. To those who listen to My teaching, more understanding will be given. But for those who are not listening, even what they think they understand will be taken away from them."

~ LUKE 8:18 NLT

Do you actually listen when friends talk with you? Or do you listen for a moment and then start thinking what your response is going to be. Do you hear the first couple of words and then shut down because you think you know what the rest of the sentence will be? Do you listen with your mind already made up?

Listening with an open mind and heart is the best way to learn. If you listen with your mind already made up, thinking that you know everything, you will not be able to learn much.

Living it

Dear Father,

If I think about how I read Your Word, I know that I'm not really listening. I read familiar passages and think, "Oh, I know that," and I don't listen to hear whatever new thing You want to teach me. I'm sorry. Help me to listen better to You and to those around me.

In Jesus' name, Amen.

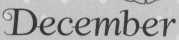

December

The Least of All

"Anyone who welcomes Me also welcomes My Father who sent Me. Whoever is the least among you is the greatest."

~ LUKE 9:48 NLT

Once again Jesus addresses how important the topic of humility is in your relationship with Him. A heart that is submitted to Jesus and therefore humble is the heart that pleases Him.

Power and importance are not impressive to Jesus. What's truly important is humility, love for others, and devotion to Jesus ... those are what make you great.

Living it

Humility is a constant topic in Jesus' teaching because it matters to Him how you relate to others. Do you notice those people who are on the fringe of your world? Are there some who are invisible to you simply because you don't know them, or they are different from you? Make time to notice them. You may receive an incredible blessing by doing so!

Know What's Important

"Martha, Martha," the Lord answered, "you are worried and upset about many things, but few things are needed – or indeed only one. Mary has chosen what is better, and it will not be taken away from her."

~ LUKE 10:41-42

The story of Mary and Martha has presented struggles to women throughout the centuries. It's good to be busy, like Martha was. She focused on preparing dinner. But she was annoyed that Mary wasn't helping her. Mary was just sitting beside Jesus and listening to what He had to say.

Martha wanted Jesus to make Mary help her. She must have been surprised that Jesus was pleased because Mary rather wanted to spend time with Him. Martha learned an important lesson that day – that spending time with Jesus and getting to know Him is more important than other trivial things.

Living it

Spending time with God is the key to our strength and success in all areas of life. Be sure that you never try to work God into your schedule, but always work your schedule around Him.

– Joyce Meyer

Amazing Love

"So I say to you: Ask and it will be given to you; seek and you will find; knock and the door will be opened to you."
~ LUKE 11:9

Jesus loves you so very much. Just read these words over again. He wants you to ask for what you need. He wants to bless you beyond anything you can imagine.

Jesus promises that God hears your prayers. He loves you and wants to give you good gifts. Ask, seek and knock, but don't neglect spending time in His Word and praying so that your requests are guided by His Spirit. He loves you so very much.

Living it

Prayer is an amazing gift. Think about it – you have the listening ear of the Creator of all things; the most powerful One in the universe. What do you do with that opportunity? Do you ask, seek and knock? Do you believe He will answer? Do you trust His answers? Pray with confidence and trust the results.

Wonderful Gifts

"If you then, though you are evil, know how to give good gifts to your children, how much more will your Father in heaven give the Holy Spirit to those who ask Him!"

~ LUKE 11:13

Jesus had just taught His followers the Lord's Prayer – a model for how to pray. Now He impresses upon them how very much God wishes to give them good gifts. The Holy Spirit is God's presence, living in their hearts, guiding, blessing and praying for them. The Holy Spirit was promised to God's people way back in the Old Testament.

The Spirit is an amazing gift to you. He lives in your heart so that God's guidance is always with you. Jesus clearly considers the Holy Spirit to be a very special gift and a grand example of God's true love for His children.

Living it

Those who belong to Christ Jesus have crucified the flesh with its passions and desires. Since we live by the Spirit, let us keep in step with the Spirit.

– Galatians 5:24-25

A Close Relationship

"Blessed rather are those who hear the Word of God and obey it."

~ LUKE 11:28

*I*n the middle of Jesus' teaching a woman in the crowd called out, "Blessed is the mother who gave You birth" and Jesus' response was this verse.

Hearing and obeying God's Word brings you closer to Jesus than having a blood relation. Hearing and obeying God's teachings in the Bible brings blessings. What kind of blessings? The blessing of knowing Jesus better and growing closer and closer to Him. Jesus wants to know you. Will you let Him?

Living it

The biblical word for "obey" comes from the Greek "*hupakou*," which means to listen attentively. This word conveys the idea of *actively* following a command. There is no choice in the matter, it is to be done whether one agrees with it or not. Obedience is involuntary.

Outside the Box

"But God said to him, 'You fool! This very night your life will be demanded from you. Then who will get what you have prepared for yourself?' This is how it will be with whoever stores up things for themselves but is not rich toward God."

~ LUKE 12:20-21

This is the end of a story Jesus told about a rich man who had so many crops that he didn't know what to do with them. But instead of sharing his crops with those who were less fortunate than himself, he built a bigger barn to store up all he had. He thought he was set for life. But his life would end that very night and he would learn that he had not pleased God by thinking only of himself instead of how he could help others.

Look around you; how can you help others? Where are the needs you can meet? Look for ways to think outside the parameters of taking care of just yourself.

Living it

Dear Father,
The world shouts that we should store up treasures for ourselves and that even if we give to others it should be out of our excess. Father, help me to give generously and with abandon. Help me to give as You give to me.

In Jesus' name, Amen.

Trusting God

Turning to His disciples, Jesus said, "That is why I tell you not to worry about everyday life – whether you have enough food to eat or enough clothes to wear. For life is more than food, and your body more than clothing."
~ LUKE 12:22-23 NLT

Of course you know that as a believer you should trust God, therefore worry is often the biggest enemy for a Christian. It's hard not to worry when things aren't going well. Worry and trust cannot live in your heart at the same time. Worry pushes everything else aside.

It's hard sometimes, but your trust in God will grow stronger and stronger, a step at a time. Trust Him for a small thing and the next bigger thing will be a little easier. Learning to trust is a major step in the journey of faith.

Living it

The faithful love of the LORD never ends! His mercies never cease. Great is His faithfulness; His mercies begin afresh each morning.
– Lamentations 3:22-23 NLT

Worry vs. Peace

"Can all your worries add a single moment to your life? And if worry can't accomplish a little thing like that, what's the use of worrying over bigger things?"

~ LUKE 12:25-26 NLT

Worry and fear cannot live in the same heart. If you nurture worry in your heart it can become like a plant that grows so quickly that it is soon out of control. You often worry about things you can't change, so ... why worry?

You can trust Jesus to take care of you because He loves you more than you can imagine. Can you trust Him to take complete care of you, every moment of every day that He gives you in this life? Trust is much more peaceful than worry.

Living it

You can't wring your hands and roll up your sleeves at the same time.

– Pat Schroeder

Misplaced Treasure

"Where your treasure is, there your heart will be also."
~ Luke 12:34

OK, it's true that love grows, right? Like when you have your first child you think you could never love a second one as much ... but you do! It is possible to love a lot of people equally. But loving many people is not the same as loving God.

It doesn't work to try and divide your heart. You can't put all your energy, thoughts and time into one thing, but then say that your heart belongs totally to God. It doesn't work. Your treasure is actually whatever occupies your time, thoughts and energy, and if it isn't knowing and serving God, then your treasure is in the wrong place. Evaluate yourself honestly ... where is your treasure today?

Living it

Dear Father,
I do struggle with this. I want to love You more than anything else. I want You to rule my life. I want to trust You completely. Father, I ask for Your help in putting You first in my heart each morning, and keeping You there all day.
In Jesus' name, Amen.

Rising to the Top

"All those who exalt themselves will be humbled, and those who humble themselves will be exalted."

~ LUKE 14:11

Pride has no place in the heart of a believer. What are symptoms of pride? The need to be number one, the center of attention, the life of the party, to be better than anyone else, to push others down in order to lift yourself up.

Jesus said if you're filled with pride in yourself, you're going to have a reality check. The people in God's kingdom who are lifted to the top are those who are humble. Those people rise to the top.

Living it

This is pretty much counter to anything you hear outside of Scripture. This is especially true at a time when women are struggling for recognition and equal benefits – and bumping against a glass ceiling. But don't let those struggles build pride in your heart that inhibits your relationships and work for Christ. Find the balance.

Count on It

"When you give a banquet, invite the poor, the crippled, the lame, the blind, and you will be blessed. Although they cannot repay you, you will be repaid at the resurrection of the righteous."
~ LUKE 14:13-14

When you have free time do you always choose to spend it with a close friend? Do you ever go outside of your comfort zone and spend time with someone with whom you aren't so comfortable?

Jesus makes the point that the woman who follows Him does not only spend time with those who are her comfortable friends. Pay attention to the people the world pushes aside. Help them. Be their friend. They may not be able to pay you back for your kindness, but Jesus will repay you one day. Count on it.

Living it

Dear Father,
I'm not sure how to go about this. Will You help me to see those in my world who I've looked past? Will You give me the courage to get to know them? I guess I'm scared of rejection and then being alone ... maybe the same things they are afraid of.
In Jesus' name, Amen.

Party On!

"There is more joy in heaven over one lost sinner who repents and returns to God than over ninety-nine others who are righteous and haven't strayed away!"

~ Luke 15:7 NLT

A party in heaven! Imagine! And it's for you! The moment you accepted Christ as your Savior a party broke out in heaven! A party ... to celebrate you! That's how much Jesus loves you.

Every time a person turns to Jesus there is a celebration in heaven. Take time to thank Jesus for celebrating you! And commit to doing your part to bring others into the Kingdom. Party on!

Living it

Though you have not seen Him, you love Him; and even though you do not see Him now, you believe in Him and are filled with an inexpressible and glorious joy, for you are receiving the end result of your faith, the salvation of your souls.

– 1 Peter 1:8-9

Celebrations

"'My son,' the father said, 'you are always with me, and everything I have is yours. But we had to celebrate and be glad,
because this brother of yours was dead and is alive again; he
was lost and is found.'"

~ LUKE 15:31-32

The story of the Prodigal Son is well known for the
son's repentance and the father's forgiveness and
grace. On the other side of that story is the older son who
stayed home and was jealous of the celebration given to
his brother. He was jealous that his father celebrated his
brother's return. He wouldn't allow himself to celebrate
his brother's homecoming.

Don't let jealousy keep you from celebrating when
someone comes to faith or has a victory or grows
stronger. Celebrate with them!

Living it

Amazing grace! (how sweet the sound)
That sav'd a wretch like me!
I once was lost, but now am found,
Was blind, but now I see.

– John Newton

No Sharing

"No one can serve two masters. Either you will hate the one and love the other, or you will be devoted to the one and despise the other. You cannot serve both God and money."

~ LUKE 16:13

A divided heart is an ineffective heart. Over and over, Jesus emphasizes that you shouldn't put a high value on money and you should think about others before yourself. The thing with money is either you have it or you don't. If you don't, then you want it. If you do, then you want more.

Money has its place, of course, to meet your needs, but it should also be shared with those who don't have enough. Getting it and keeping it should never be more important than God. He will not share your heart with anyone or anything. Make God Number One.

Living it

Choose my instruction instead of silver, knowledge rather than choice gold, for wisdom is more precious than rubies, and nothing you desire can compare with her.

– Proverbs 8:10-11

Saying Thanks

"Were not all ten cleansed? Where are the other nine?"
~ LUKE 17:17

Jesus often invited His followers to pray. Prayer offers us a great opportunity to share what's on our heart with God. But just as you appreciate being thanked when you do something for someone else, it's a good idea to thank God, too, to show your gratitude for His answers to prayer.

Ten men who had leprosy called out to Jesus. Ten men asked Him to heal them. Ten men believed He could. Jesus healed them and sent them to show the priests that they had been healed. One man came back to say thank you. Nine did not. Only one man praised God for the miracle of healing.

Saying thank you is important. When Jesus does something for you, take time to thank Him.

Living it

Give thanks in all circumstances; for this is God's will for you in Christ Jesus.
– 1 Thessalonians 5:18

Heart Kingdom

"The coming of the kingdom of God is not something that can be observed, nor will people say, 'Here it is,' or 'There it is,' because the kingdom of God is in your midst."

~ LUKE 17:20-21

It is within you. The Holy Spirit dwells in your heart. His power, love and guidance is there for you. One day God's kingdom will be a physical reality, but for now the Kingdom is in the midst of a group of believers, praying together, worshiping, serving and sharing their faith. Don't neglect joining together with other believers. There is strength and encouragement in being together.

Living it

Dear Father,
It's humbling to know that Your Spirit dwells in me. Yet I know I couldn't make it without Him. I pray, Father, that others will see Your kingdom in me. And, in seeing it, will desire it to be in their own lives.

In Jesus' name, Amen.

Be Still

"Let the little children come to Me, and do not hinder them,
for the kingdom of God belongs to such as these. Truly I tell
you, anyone who will not receive the kingdom of God like a
little child will never enter it."
~ LUKE 18:16-17

*L*ife gets heavy at times. It sometimes seems as though
problems come in waves and you are gasping for air
in between them. The stress and fear of those times make
the humility and childlike faith that Jesus is talking
about here even more important.

Even (or especially) in the middle of your trials, it is
important to have time alone with God. Tell Him what's
on your heart, then just be still before Him and let Him
soothe your troubled heart. Ask Him to grow your faith
to be like a child's, based on humility, trust and
dependence on Jesus.

Living it

Childlike faith focuses on our heavenly Father, not on our
fears.
– Anonymous

Come ... Follow Me

"You still lack one thing. Sell everything you have and give to the poor, and you will have treasure in heaven. Then come, follow Me."

~ LUKE 18:22

Some stories are repeated in all four Gospels, with different emphasis in each case. The repetitive emphasis with the story of the rich man who asked Jesus how to obtain eternal life is what's important.

Make your choice – do you truly care about knowing and serving Jesus, or is your "stuff" more important than Him? Jesus will not just be fit into your life around other people and activities. He wants all of your heart. That may require some things that are difficult – such as the rich man giving away his wealth – but it is worth it because the invitation is there ... "Come, follow Me," Jesus invites us.

Living it

The "stuff" you've spent your life acquiring may be getting in the way of a blessed, pure, beautiful relationship with God. Don't let it be more important than knowing Him.

Holding Nothing Back

"I tell you the truth," Jesus said, "this poor widow has given more than all the rest of them. For they have given a tiny part of their surplus, but she, poor as she is, has given everything she has."

~ LUKE 21:3-4 NLT

*T*his is a beautiful story of a woman who held nothing back from God's work. She had so little but she gave sacrificially, trusting God to take care of her. It's a bit scary to think of living sacrificially, giving to God's work so that others can have the bare necessities.

It's a step of faith to trust God to take care of any unexpected needs you might have and that you might be saving toward. Are you holding back from God? Your money? Your energy? Your time? Your prayers? He notices – as we know, Jesus noticed the gentle widow who gave her all.

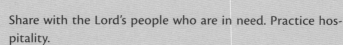

Living it

Share with the Lord's people who are in need. Practice hospitality.

– Romans 12:13

Living Water

"If you knew the gift of God and who it is that asks you for a drink, you would have asked Him and He would have given you living water."

~ JOHN 4:10

*L*iving water. Think about that for a moment – water that nourishes not just your body but your soul. Water that can wash away the grime on your hands and face, and in your heart. Water that brings a fullness of life you never imagined.

It comes from Jesus and its supply never runs out. Sounds good, right? This amazing, life-giving water is right in front of you. Grab it by giving your heart to Jesus and allowing that river to flow into your heart ... through Him.

Living it

Cleanse me with hyssop, and I will be clean; wash me, and I will be whiter than snow.

– Psalm 51:7

Everyone Has a Job to Do

"Thus the saying, 'One sows and another reaps' is true. I sent you to reap what you have not worked for. Others have done the hard work, and you have reaped the benefits of their labor."

~ JOHN 4:37-38

Saving the world is not all on your shoulders. The work of God is done through teamwork. Each person has different gifts, talents and opportunities.

Some people are really good at explaining the pathway to salvation, some at just being friends with people, some are good counselors, and others are good teachers.

It takes everyone playing a part for one person to come to Jesus. So, one person may plant a seed, but someone else will lead that person to faith. Enjoy your role on the team.

Living it

I challenge you to think of one act of genuine significance in the history of humankind that was performed by a lone human being (apart from the redemptive work of Christ on the cross). No matter what you name, you will find that a team of people was involved.

– John C. Maxwell

Spiritual Food

"I am the Bread of Life. Whoever comes to Me will never go hungry, and whoever believes in Me will never be thirsty."

~ JOHN 6:35

*B*read is nourishment for the body. Nourishment helps your body grow and develop into adulthood. Accordingly, nourishment keeps it healthy, energetic and strong.

Jesus, as the Bread of Life, does those same things for your soul – growing and developing it and helping you become the woman He wants you to be. Don't neglect partaking of this Bread of Life. Spend time alone with Jesus, praying, listening, waiting. Let Him nourish your soul.

Living it

Speaking the truth in love, we will grow to become in every respect the mature body of Him who is the Head, that is, Christ.

– Ephesians 4:15

Slavery

"I tell you the truth, everyone who sins is a slave of sin."
~ JOHN 8:34 NLT

Have you admitted or accepted your sin of slavery? Is there that one sin that keeps you locked in solitary confinement? Have you acknowledged it? Overeating, selfishness, pride?

Sin becomes so attractive that once you give in to that one temptation, it is very hard to stop. Without really thinking about it, your favorite sin becomes a habit. Then, after a while, that one sin isn't enough and you begin to do more. Sin is addictive and can quickly make you a slave. Stop the process. Confess your weakness and ask God to free you from its power.

Living it

Dear Father,
I've ignored it. I've justified it. I've lied about it. Now, I face it. I confess my bondage to sin – this one that I can't seem to let go of. Help me to gain victory over it. Help me to bring it to You each time it rears its ugly head. Thank You for your strength.
In Jesus' name, Amen.

The Good Shepherd

"I am the Good Shepherd. The Good Shepherd lays down His life for the sheep."

~ JOHN 10:11

In the dark of night, amidst the trials of life, you may feel alone. It may seem that you're fighting to survive, searching to find your way and no one is helping or guiding you.

It's simply not so. Jesus *is* your Good Shepherd. A shepherd's job is 24/7, because sheep wander away if they aren't watched. The shepherd must find food and water for His flock and protect them from predators. Jesus is your Shepherd. He's always on duty ... watching, leading, protecting. You need not ever feel alone.

Living it

What is a shepherd's job? It is to watch out for his sheep, to take them to food and water and to protect them from harm. Jesus will do these things for you. He is the Bread of Life and the Living Water, which will nourish your soul. He will protect you from Satan's tricks. Jesus laid down His life to protect you. You are never alone.

Knowing God

"If you really know Me, you will know My Father as well. From now on, you do know Him and have seen Him."
~ JOHN 14:7

*D*oesn't it just blow your mind that you can actually *know* God, the Creator of the universe? It must have stunned Jesus' disciples. They had traveled with Him and saw Him do amazing miracles, yet they knew Him as human. Now He tells them that by knowing Him they also know God!

The only way anyone can truly know God is by knowing Jesus. He is the bridge to God and by getting to know Him, you learn to know God better. It does take time. It also takes faith and trust, but yes, you can actually *know* God.

Living it

Dear Father,
The only thing I can say is ... thank You. What a privilege to know You. What a sacrifice it took to make it possible. May I never, ever take this honor lightly.
In Jesus' name, Amen.

Friends with Jesus

"You are My friends if you do what I command."

~ JOHN 15:14

People don't generally put conditions on their friends. So, why does Jesus? He does so because He is not only your friend; He is your role model for how to live, how to serve God, how to love others. He wants the best for you.

His motive is to grow in intimacy with you and that growth will come as you obey Him more and more. It's a process of growing and learning and the reward for that is friendship with Jesus.

Living it

Lord, whatever you want, wherever you want it, and whenever you want it, that's what I want.

– Richard Baxter

A Close-Knit Family

"I am praying not only for these disciples but also for all who will ever believe in Me through their message. I pray that they will all be one, just as You and I are one – as You are in Me, Father, and I am in You. And may they be in Us so that the world will believe You sent Me."

~ JOHN 17:20-21 NLT

It's so sad when Christians disagree. Especially when their arguments are over things that have no importance in the realm of eternity. Jesus prayed for unity with other believers. All who call Jesus their Savior are in His family.

When Christians argue and criticize one another, it takes attention away from the message of Jesus' love for the world. It certainly doesn't make life as a believer attractive to those you're trying to bring to faith. Jesus prayed that His followers would live in unity with one another and with Him and God. That's the best way for unbelievers to see the truth of His love.

Living it

How good and pleasant it is when God's people live together in unity!

– Psalm 133:1

Everything Changed

"Put your sword away! Shall I not drink the cup the Father has given Me?"

~ JOHN 18:11

*I*t was the beginning of the end. Soldiers had come to arrest Jesus and one of His followers pulled out a sword to defend Him. Jesus stopped His friend because He knew He was doing what God wanted Him to do. He knew it was going to be hard – He would be tortured and murdered – but it was God's plan for Him. Jesus was completely surrendered to the plan ... because of His love for you.

The temptation, as your faith becomes a way of life through the years, may be to forget how very special this sacrificial choice was. Don't forget. It changed everything.

Living it

Imitate God, therefore, in everything you do, because you are His dear children. Live a life filled with love, following the example of Christ. He loved us and offered Himself as a sacrifice for us, a pleasing aroma to God.

– Ephesians 5:1-2

Peace

Jesus came and stood among them and said, "Peace be with you!"

~ JOHN 20:26

Do you have peace in your life? There are times when peace seems unattainable, yet Jesus often said, "Peace be with you." Even in the middle of terrible circumstances, such as after His own crucifixion, He came to His followers and said, "Peace be with you." How could He expect them to have peace at a time like that?

How can you have peace? You can't without trust and faith that Jesus has a plan and that nothing that happens to you surprises Him. The pathway to peace is marked by faith and trust in Jesus.

Living it

The peace of God, which transcends all understanding, will guard your hearts and your minds in Christ Jesus.

– Philippians 4:7

Growing Faith

"Because you have seen Me, you have believed; blessed are those who have not seen and yet have believed."

~ JOHN 20:29

Thomas just couldn't, or wouldn't, believe that Jesus had actually come back to life after being murdered. He needed to see Jesus for himself. When he did, he believed.

Jesus gives a special blessing to the thousands of others throughout history who have not actually seen Him or touched Him, yet have believed that He lives. It takes an active faith to believe without seeing. Jesus blesses you for that faith and will help your faith grow stronger and stronger, if you just believe in Him.

Living it

Dear Father,
Some people say that I "fight" my way to faith. It would be so much easier to just believe. But I don't know how, so please show me how to believe without seeing or arguing ... just to believe in faith.

In Jesus' name, Amen.

Shepherd's Work

Jesus said, "Feed My sheep."
~ JOHN 21:17

You have a partnership with Jesus in His work on earth. He wants you to feed His sheep. Three times Jesus asked Peter if he truly loved Him. Three times Peter replied, "You know I love You." Finally Jesus told Peter to feed His sheep.

What does that mean? It means that Jesus' followers should continue teaching what Jesus taught. You are to help believers grow stronger in faith by using the opportunities and talents He has given you.

Sometimes that means stepping out of your comfort zone. Sometimes it means doing things you'd really rather not do. But it's Jesus' work – and what a privilege to be a part of it.

Living it

I am certain that God, who began the good work within you, will continue His work until it is finally finished on the day when Christ Jesus returns.
– Philippians 1:6 NLT

About the Author

Carolyn Larsen is an author, actress, and an experienced speaker with a God-given passion for ministering to women and children. She has spoken at conferences and retreats around the United States, Canada, and India. Carolyn has written over 40 books for children and adults. Carolyn lives in Glen Ellyn, Illinois, with her husband, Eric. They have three children.